Chakras

Chakras

JOURNEY THROUGH
THE ENERGY CENTRES
OF YOUR BODY

DR RAVI RATAN & DR MINOO RATAN

ROCKPOOL

A Rockpool book
PO Box 252
Summer Hill
NSW 2130
Australia

rockpoolpublishing.com
Follow us! **f** **@** rockpoolpublishing
Tag your images with #rockpoolpublishing

ISBN: 9781922785435

Originally published in 2007 by the Institute of
Holistic Health Sciences, Mumbai, India

Second edition published in 2019 by Rockpool Publishing

This edition published in 2023 by Rockpool Publishing

Design and typesetting by Daniel Poole, Rockpool Publishing
Edited by Lisa Macken

A catalogue record for this
book is available from the
National Library of Australia

Printed and bound in China
10 9 8 7 6 5 4 3 2 1

About the authors

Dr Ravi Ratan,
MSc, MBA, DSc

Dr Ravi Ratan, from Mumbai, India, is a clinical aromatherapist who integrates aromatherapy with manual lymphatic drainage, emotional release and chakra healing. Born into a Hindu Brahmin family, he was brought up in Hindu spiritual traditions and followed spiritual practices and rituals as part of his upbringing. He has a lineage of doctors, teachers and healers in the family, and was exposed to yoga and meditations early in his life with various teachers and masters. He has incorporated all this learning into his integrated healing practice.

Dr Ravi achieved his Masters in Science (Zoology) and Masters in Business Management in the late 1970s while quite young. He started his career in administration, then moved on to start his own perfumery business in India. While blending aromatic oils and products for perfumery, he realised the healing potential of natural plant essential oils. He found working with essential oils for health and healing more fulfilling, and shifted his focus to aromatherapy. He developed his own range of aromatherapy products for the skin and hair and general well-being in 1993, and started sharing his knowledge of plant essential oils and their therapeutic effects through his training workshops first in India and now worldwide. His documented healing work with essential plant oils earned him a DSc (Medicina Alternativa) from the Open International University of Alternative Medicine (recognised by the World Health Organization). Part of that healing experience had been incorporated in his Handbook of Aromatherapy (Institute of Holistic Health Sciences, 2006).

Dr Ravi and his wife have been associated with various spiritual teachers and masters from whom they received the knowledge and understanding of the chakras, the chakra system and kriya yoga for chakra healing. Their workshops on the chakras and chakra healing demystify the existence of the chakras, the relevance of various attributes and the process of disease. They have integrated chakra healing with aromatherapy, manual lymph drainage and emotional release work. This book is an effort to share this understanding with the world.

Dr Minoo Ratan
MSc, BEd, PhD

Dr Minoo Ratan, the wife of Dr Ravi, is a life coach, practising psycho-aromatherapist and healer. In her psychotherapy practice she integrates aromatherapy with lymph drainage and chakra healing.

Dr Minoo has a Masters in Psychology and specialisation in occupational stress, besides a degree in education focusing on adolescent stress. She started treating psychosomatic conditions using plant essential oils in 1993. She submitted successful case studies as part of her research, for which she was awarded her PhD by the Open International University of Alternative Medicine. She is also a member of Bombay Psychology Association and has been trained in advanced pranic healing with psychotherapy and eye movement desensitisation and reprocessing (based on the Shapiro School, USA) for trauma management.

Dr Minoo's Mind Body Clinic is in Mumbai, India, where she provides consultancy and counselling and life coaching for the management of psychosomatic disorders as well as interpersonal problems. She also provides healing treatments using aromatherapy, manual lymph drainage, chakra therapy and pranic and spiritual healings. She has an association with institutions such as Dr BMN College of Home Science and MMP Shah College, both in Mumbai, as a counsellor, also conducting various training workshops for students and other institutions on stress management, inner grooming, chakra healing and meditation and naam sankirtan yoga.

Dr Minoo travels to the USA, Canada, the UK, Europe and Australia to offer consultancy and treatments, as well as co-conducting training workshops on integrated healing with aromatherapy, lymph drainage, emotional release and chakra healing with Dr Ravi Ratan. They also use healing crystals and wand therapy.

For more information please visit www.aromatantra.com

Guru Brahma
Guru Vishnu
Guru Devo Maheshwaraiya
Guru Sakashat Per Brahma
Tasme Shri Guruveyah Namah

'No spiritual progress is possible without the guidance of the guru.'

This book is dedicated to our gurus.

Dedication

'Our first gurus [teachers] are our parents; during our upbringing our parents and family elders give us sanskar, the basic values of life. Learning comes to us through books, journals, television, the internet and social media, which provide information and answers to our questions. When we are open to learning everyone is our teacher, some we actively seek and some we draw into our lives; when the seeker is ready, guru appears. Often we learn simply by observing others even though they may be unaware of that, so that even our students and clients are our teachers. Guru is not just a physical body but is our guiding principle.'

— Om Shri Gurave Namaha

Contents

Acknowledgements

This book couldn't have been completed without the blessings and guidance of our gurus. The universal guru (or the guiding principle) has been there for all of us to guide us all the time; he is the one who moulds our thoughts and perception, and gives ideas and knowledge. There are also gurus who are embodied; in our case we have the grace of Shree Shivkrupanand Swami and Dr Jayant Balaji Athawale and many more.

The chakras are described in so many books, none of which give a complete understanding. So many reference books, interactions and queries with our gurus, students and clients has helped give us an understanding of the subject, for which there still isn't any authentic literature.

The subject of chakras covers all aspects of our lives, physical, mental, emotional and spiritual. The process of growing up is in fact a journey through the chakras for a child. During the process of growing he or she goes through various phases of life, during which a particular chakra will be dominant and play a definite role in the development of physical and physiological organs and emotional development. Today we are more aware of the external world and the gadgets we use, but not so much aware of the way our own bodies work and how they process feelings and emotions. Tantra highlights those aspects of life such as breath and movement of energies, which medical science doesn't delve into but which the fields of yoga and Ayurveda give a lot of importance to.

The authors were blessed to have been born in the Hindu tradition and into a spiritual family. Our universal guru ensured we received guidance not only from our personal gurus but that we were also exposed to modern and scientific aspects related to the subject of chakras through our interactions with friends and students and feedback from our associates. John S. Rogerson introduced us to the ISIS photo energy field imaging system, which enabled us to authenticate our energy-healing results.

We are thankful to our parents, whose guidance has helped us throughout our lives. We are also thankful to our daughters Vartika and Kartikeya for their help, interest and support in the completion of this book.

The word 'chakra' has so much mysticism about it, and in recent times more and more people have felt drawn to the subject. However, in the absence of any authentic literature there are misconceptions about the role, numbers and locations of the individual chakras. Most of the knowledge and understanding about chakras has percolated down from various teachers, sages and philosophers, and is contained in ancient Hindu texts such as the Vedas and Upanishads and books on yoga and tantra. These all give reference to the subject, but the information is available in bits and pieces and is generally associated with particular attributes or practices rather than providing the whole picture.

The objective of this book is to offer maximum information and clarity on the subject of chakras and their associated attributes and practices, not to promote the Hindu religion. Since most of the information on the subject has come from ancient Hindu traditions and rituals followed in tantra and other spiritual practices, we have given references and explanations of those as well as taking scientific and metaphysical perspectives into consideration.

Often people vaguely refer to chakras as 'energy centres on the body' and then add their own understanding and vision of the role they play in our lives. The medical community may not understand chakras unless the practitioner has a spiritual inclination or background. In medical schools studies are done on cadavers, which don't have energy and vibrations so it is beyond their scope. Chakras are the subject of living beings, because only living beings have vibrations and energy.

We describe chakras as energy centres because they are the result of energy metabolism in the body, representing the activity of our organs and glands. Different spiritual and healing traditions talk of different numbers of chakras: 7, 9, 12 or 14 and up to 108 chakras. The fact is, wherever there is an energy activity a chakra is present. We have restricted the scope of this book to the seven major chakras, as mentioned in kundalini tantra. These seven are located on the torso and head, the parts of the body housing our vital organs and glands. From a health perspective, understanding the association of chakras with our organs and glands gives an insight into the process of disease.

We have discussed chakras from tantric, spiritual, metaphysical and health perspectives. The focus of this book is not kundalini work or promoting kundalini awakening practices, which should be done under the guidance of a teacher with awakened kundalini. We are health practitioners, and our focus has been to create an understanding of the subject purely from a health perspective.

According to kundalini tantra the human body is composed of three layers, which are also described as bodies. The first layer is the physical body, which is enveloped by an energetic layer called the subtle body, while the outermost layer enveloping both of these is known as our causal body. These bodies function as the vehicle for the inner self or the soul. The latter two are energetic layers or vibratory fields embodying the underlying consciousness.

Our physical body, the result of the sexual union of our parents, is the one we normally experience and sustain with food. Our awareness within this body constitutes the waking state of consciousness, and is made up of 16 components: five sensory organs (eyes/sight, ears/hearing, tongue/taste, skin/touch, nose/smell); five organs of action (feet, hands, rectum, genitals, mouth); five elements (earth, water, air, fire, ether); and the mind.

The energetic basis or pure form of the physical body is the subtle body, sometimes called the aura; it is also composed of 16 components. Within the subtle body exist the seven major chakras, which get fully activated with the force of kundalini shakti. Finally, there is the more ethereal body known as the causal body (karana sharira), the creative force behind the other two bodies. In fact, the causal body forms an egg shape around the other two bodies. These three bodies are linked with one another through the chakras, or energy centres.

'Chakra' is a Sanskrit word that relates to a wheel; in tantric context this term is used to describe the wheels of energy associated with our subtle bodies. In ancient texts such as the Vedas and Upanishads, there is very little reference to the term kundalini and chakras as most of the knowledge on this subject had been passed on through guru-shisya (teacher-disciple) lineage. Finding an authentic literature on the subject can be difficult, though there has been reference to chakras in tantric, yogic and Ayurvedic texts.

Hindu philosophy attaches as much importance to the mind and the soul as to the body. According to kundalini tantra we have a physical body and an energy body. Chakras, the vortices of spinning energy, are the parts of our energy bodies that are in continuous interplay with universal energy. Energy is neutral and is shaped through our mental and emotional processes, the expression of thoughts, speech and action. Though described as energy centres of our bodies, our chakras represent the activity of organs and glands. They are actually the transfer points of our thoughts and emotions and the physical functioning of specific organs and endocrine glands. When our chakras are balanced we feel grounded and centred, and have self-discipline.

According to Ayurveda, our health is the sum total of our lifestyle practices. We have to find balance between our physical, nutritional, mental/emotional and spiritual lifestyles. An imbalance in our lifestyles and a lack of discipline lead to chakra imbalances and health issues. Ancient teachings tell us that all human actions originate in the mind, thus our mental/emotional state affects our energy levels. Prolonged mental and emotional stress affects our energies in a negative way, lowers our immune system and causes health issues. When our emotions are blocked our chakras also become dull and sluggish, affecting the flow of energy; this can later manifest as a disease of the organs and glands associated with the particular chakras.

In our healing practices, the main objective is to assess the imbalance in a person's lifestyle to identify the cause of disease and help correct it with the right practices. We are all aware that mental/emotional circumstances have a major influence on a person's health and find most imbalances and blockages coming from that area. We call it 'mind over body' or psychosomatics. In today's world, a vast number of health practitioners are working on restoring health by healing the mind and emotions. Through counselling we try to explain how greatly negative thoughts and emotions affect people, but sometimes it's difficult to change the thinking processes and temperament. There is still something beyond us that needs to be dealt with, and that is the higher mind. This higher mind has to be worked on at a subtle level, which is where living a spiritual lifestyle helps. All spiritual books and guides suggest we are energy bodies and we are connected to the source, which is the consciousness of God.

From a spiritual perspective, chakras are best understood as levels of discrimination, not morality. Tantra also associates gunas (levels of consciousness) to chakras; the three gunas are known as tamas, rajas and sattva. It is said that our physical bodies are the carriers of the soul or our individual consciousness. Our individual consciousness came to this physical body through the crown or sahasrara chakra and goes all the way down to settle at the end of the spine as our kundalini shakti, activating the muladhara or base root chakra. We have been born into a material world, where everybody is largely chasing physical objects and desires as our consciousness is stuck in this material world. There is so much more to life than fame, fortune, status, authority and attachments to people and things. Pain comes to us through ignorance and being blind when experience tells us something different. Impurities of the mind need to be understood from the perspective of discrimination rather than morality. Impurities arise out of greed, desire, self-gratification and self-interest; however, spiritual practices will lead us to a path of righteousness and working beyond the self, which helps raise our level of consciousness from our root chakra upwards.

We often know much more about the outside world than we do about our own being, about how the body, mind and spirit work in conjunction and how we are affected by our mental and emotional states and temperament. In this book we cover various attributes associated with chakras and health, and we also explain the process of disease. Chakra healing is a vibrational healing that helps the mind, body and spirit. We can also use various healing tools such as essential oils, crystals, yoga, chanting and meditation to complement the energy work.

As aromatherapists we are particularly focused on essential oils, which are also known as the pranas of the plant. Their high vibrations and therapeutic benefits, combined with lymph drainage, have an amazing ability to unblock, heal and balance chakras, so we have devoted an entire chapter to explain how to utilise these tools to improve health or healing practice. Healing work is mainly intuitive, and we expect practitioners to rely on their intuition besides using the healing tool of their preference. The path of healing and spirituality is fairly subjective and each individual's experience will differ. We do not expect all readers to subscribe to or endorse our views.

1

The chakra system

A system is a complex mechanism of interacting, interdependent components forming an intricate whole. In a similar way, chakras are interdependent, intricate and complicated mechanisms of the body that should be understood as a complete system. Ayurveda and tantra associate various attributes to each individual chakra, which affect chakras' functioning at energetic and physiological levels. To understand the proper functioning of the chakra system we need to understand each attribute and its effect on chakras as well as on the whole being.

From a health and healer's perspective, chakras are the barometer of our health. In different healing modalities or spiritual practices there could be a variation in the numbers and location of the chakras;

however, they may all be correct from their understanding of major and minor chakras. According to kundalini tantra there are seven major chakras located on our torsos and heads representing the activity of vital organs and glands. These seven major chakras are the focal point of this book. The activity and balance of our chakras reflect the health of our organs and glands. While in modern medicine cadavers are studied in order to understand health and disease, in chakra healing we need to study living beings: their physical, nutritional, mental and emotional life styles.

To understand chakras, we need to understand human life and its evolution. Evolution is a universal process; all life is evolving and humankind is no exception. Life, creation and evolution are the stages in the unfolding of consciousness. We as human beings are evolving, not only as individuals but also as a race. The muladhara or base root chakra is our most fundamental chakra; from here our process of evolution in this lifetime begins, culminating at sahasrara — the crown chakra.

The **muladhara** chakra corresponds to the coccygeal plexus and is located at the perineum (between the anus and the genitals), the spot that touches the ground when we sit in the lotus position. As the name suggests (mul: root; adhar: base), this chakra is the foundation of the physical body in the realm of physical existence. During the process of spiritual evolution, a person goes through animal consciousness and then on to be a real human. There are certain minor chakras from

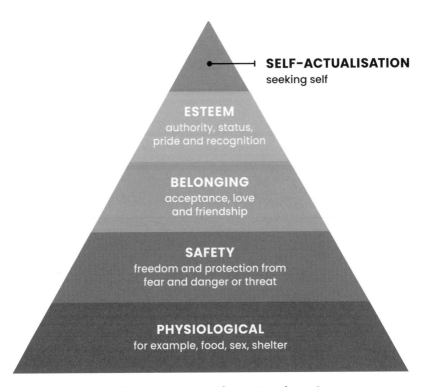

Abraham Maslow's hierarchy of needs

muladhara down to the heels that are responsible for the development of animal and human instincts as well as intellect. Muladhara is responsible for survival and maintenance of the physical body, and besides being a source of physical energy it also regulates all excretory functions.

Located at the pubic area or at the lowest point of the spinal column, corresponding to our sacral plexus of nerves, is the second major chakra, known as **swadhisthana** or the sacral chakra. This chakra is the desire centre of the body and the seat of emotions, hence it is responsible for emotional balance, sexuality, procreation and the exchange of sexual energy, and it also controls the unconscious in human beings.

The third major chakra is **manipura** or the solar plexus chakra, in the naval region. It corresponds to the solar plexus. Located in the V of the ribcage below the diaphragm, it controls the entire process of digestion, assimilation and temperature regulation in the body. This chakra is responsible for mental power and self-will, and is associated with our ambitions towards money, power and authority; it is known to be the seat of ego.

The first three chakras take care of our basic needs, as described by renowned psychologist Abraham Maslow in his hierarchy of needs. Only after fulfilment of the basic needs can a person focus on self-actualisation. In spiritual and tantric practices it is said that while we are stuck in the mundane and struggling with the basic needs, kundalini keeps rising up to the manipura chakra then returns to the muladhara (base root) chakra. However, once the kundalini crosses the astral bridge, which is an energetic barrier between manipura and the anahata (heart) chakra, kundalini movement is upwards only. This movement of kundalini is associated with the evolution of consciousness.

The **anahata** chakra is located at the centre of the chest, at the level of the depression of the sternum. It corresponds to the cardiac plexus of nerves and regulates the functioning of the heart, lungs, thymus gland, diaphragm and other organs in this region of the body. This is the first chakra on the path of self-actualisation and a stepping stone to spiritual growth. It is an important chakra for all healers, denoting unconditional love and empathy for all.

Our **vishuddhi** or throat chakra is located in the deep of the throat and corresponds to the cervical plexus of nerves. Responsible for communication and self-expression, it regulates the entire thyroid complex, certain systems of articulation and the upper palate and epiglottis.

Yogis and tantrics believe that the **ajna**, or third eye chakra, is located between the brows in the forehead. It is the seat of the guru — our guiding principle — and works as the command centre. It has complete control over all the functions of a disciple's life.

The aforesaid six chakras serve as triggers of energy to different parts of the brain, and are channelled through various nadis (conduits of energy, or prana). According to kundalini tantra there are two higher illuminated centres, called bindu and sahasrara. The *bindu* is located at the top back of the head and is where Hindu Brahmins keep a tuft of hair; this feeds the optic nerve and is considered to be the seat of nectar or ama-kala, the true philosopher's stone of immortality.

The *sahasrara* is supreme, the seat of higher awareness; it is is located slightly above the fontanelle. Considered to be the seventh major chakra, sahasrara is our connection to higher consciousness, the point of culmination of kundalini.

During the process of evolution, sometimes our outer experiences get in the way of our inner experiences. Known in Hindi as anubhuti, this inner experience results from our spiritual practices and is very subjective, as each seeker may get a different anubhuti in spite of carrying out the same spiritual practice. When the chakras get activated through our spiritual practices our values and perception of life also change, resulting in the improvement of the quality of love, relationships and compassion. For a yogi, the world remains the same but the perception of the world changes, resulting in sat-chit-anand, a state of eternal peace and bliss within.

Nature and consciousness

Our cosmos is the body of the Absolute (an essential attribute of God; ultimate reality), the vessel through which the Absolute expresses itself. There are two fundamental principles of the universe — nature and consciousness — that are continuously interplaying in the cosmic drama of the universe. They are basically two sides of the same coin; they are yin and yang. Supreme consciousness is the masculine principle or purusha: it is all-pervading, it is the sustainer and the only sign of divinity. Consciousness is the ultimate, out of which and by whose power mind and matter proceed. The other aspect, nature, is the feminine principle (prakriti shakti); it is the material form of the consciousness and is the one responsible for procreation. Consciousness, which exists in all forms of life, does not differentiate between people or species. It is the very basis of creation, the power of evolution.

The consciousness of a living being is conditioned by the matter that makes up this body. As long as we have a physical body we participate in the play of nature; that is maya, which is the illusionary world of desires: the desires we chase, the material things we want for illusionary happiness. As you fulfil one desire you will find you have another one, creating a vicious cycle or a web. No incarnate body can be completely worldly or completely spiritual. No matter what level of light or spirituality you attain, as long as you are embodied you are not able to transcend your dark side. The expression of shakti in the physical body is prana, the vital life force, which keeps the body, mind and spirit working as a complete whole.

The ancient law of microcosm (part) and macrocosm (whole) explains that there is no real difference between the vast external universe and the limited internal universe of the human body, except that we as individuals believe ourselves to be different. A human being is a living microcosm of the universe, and the universe is a living macrocosm of a human being. Each cosmos affects the other. Our universe affects us each moment, and each one of us also influences the entire universe by our actions. Humankind, as microcosm, contains within itself all the elements:

mineral, vegetable and animal kingdom (flora and fauna). Also, within plants is the potential of human beings, and within human beings is the underlying energy structure of plants. Life is rational, interdependent and interconnected, like an ecosystem, for mutual nourishment and care. Independence and individuality are myths of human origin: humankind cannot live without air; air exists because of the planetary mass of the Earth: the Earth exists because of the sun; the sun exists as part of the galaxy; the galaxy exists as part of the macrocosm.

In essence, both cosmic and individual consciousness are one. While the power of cosmic consciousness, chiti shakti, identifies with the unmanifested absolute, the power of individual consciousness, maya shakti, identifies with the world and is the manifestation of the absolute. As individual consciousness is a partial expression of cosmic consciousness, the two aspects cannot exist without each other; there is a spark of the absolute in even the densest of matter, which is why a rock is considered alive as it has vibrations. Similarly, in the highest state of consciousness there is a particle of maya or a sense of individuality, because the physical form identifies with the material world only. Once you understand the truth of the universe you forget your own individuality and remember your true nature. The one exists in all and all defines the one; unity and duality both exist simultaneously. Wherever chiti shakti is displayed there is intelligence and sensation. Without it there is ignorance and insensitivity.

Our bodies are our soulmates, as they are the carriers of our souls. They are like vessels, getting filled with the flow of consciousness. The chief centres of consciousness in human beings are found in the cerebrospinal system, the upper brain and hypothalamus; this is the first part of the body to be developed after conception. After that our sahasrara or crown chakra opens. Individual consciousness flows in the body through the sahasrara chakra, bringing with it a complete blueprint of our life. This blueprint is our destiny in this lifetime. According to Hindu philosophy, this destiny is based on the karma of our past lives. When a person consults an astrologer, palmist or numerologist they will try to analyse this blueprint to predict the person's destiny, although this destiny cannot be changed.

From the cerebrospinal system, entire body form materialises. The spine and spinal cord extend consciousness from the brain, the seat of highest awareness (ajna or third eye chakra), to the coccyx, the pole of greatest density (muladhara or base root chakra). This consciousness, which came through the sahasrara (crown) chakra, flows all the way down, activating the muladhara chakra so that the physical body starts taking shape.

Our individual consciousness, called our kundalini shakti, moves in sushumna nadi, one of the major energy channels running parallel to the spine. This energy is also our personal fragment of the cosmic power, for self-identification, represented as our ego or I-ness or ahamkara. While discrimination is the main characteristic of intellect, possessiveness is the chief characteristic of ego and self-identifies with every cell of our body from conception until death.

Kundalini moves in us all, rising from the muladhara (base root) chakra to the manipura (solar plexus) chakra and then going down. Since our lower three chakras are associated with the fulfilment of basic needs for survival in this material world, as long as our consciousness remains entrenched in the mundane, which is the material world, our kundalini moves in the lower three chakras.

However, once we start detaching ourselves from the material things in life and develop discretion, our spiritual awakening takes place and kundalini moves beyond manipura to the anahata (heart) chakra, crossing the subtle barrier called the astral bridge. Then its movement is only upwards. This process is called kundalini awakening, and it represents the awakening of the consciousness. This also triggers our spiritual awakening. Even if we leave our physical body at that point and take rebirth, the kundalini starts its journey from that point onwards or from the chakra to which we have already evolved. We do not remember our previous life nor do we have a realisation about the state of our kundalini, but it is evident from the existence of things such as child prodigies and xenoglossy, or the ability to speak a language without having learned it.

The more we identify with our individuality and are attached to the material things in life the more we are stuck in the lower chakras, living in the world of maya. On the other hand, when we develop detachment and identify less with our individuality, our consciousness level changes and we reflect more of the macrocosm, reflecting our chiti shakti. Maya shakti keeps us awake to the world but asleep to the absolute, while chiti shakti keeps us awake to the absolute away from worldly matters.

2

Energy

Our universe is the interplay of both manifested and unmanifested energy, thus creating a vibrational field. In fact, everything in this universe is energy. Scientifically speaking, matter, whether living or non-living, is made up of atoms and molecules. Atoms have a nucleus made up of one or more protons (with a positive charge) and a similar number of neutrons. One or more electrons (with a negative charge) are bound to the nucleus. Here we are talking about energy at its most basic level of existence. What differentiates between things in this universe is the level of the energy and the vibrational field. All forms are manifested energy mass. Human energy is also the manifestation of universal energy; it can thus be defined as a luminous body that surrounds and interpenetrates the physical body.

The concept of universal energy has been recognised and accepted through the ages by all cultures; it is omnipresent and in continuous interplay with human energy. Human energy represents our subtle body or the energy body; it is also called the bio-plasmic body. Ancient Indian seers call this energy prana, the basic constituent and source of all life. In Chinese philosophy it is called chi, while in Kabbalah, the Jewish mystical theosophy, it is referred to as astral lights. All other spiritual and religious traditions mention auric layers that are depicted as light around holy or evolved people. Christian religious paintings portray Jesus and other spiritual figures surrounded by fields of light. An aura is that part of the energy field associated with objects; when it is associated with the human body it is called a human aura. Modern advances in science have made it easy for us to understand the whole concept of energy as we now have devices that can measure energy and vibrations and take aura pictures.

Many Western scientific minds believe that a universal energy pervades all of nature, with records of this perceived energy being found in Pythagorean literature as early as 500 BCE. As reported by 12th-century scholars Boirac and Liébeault, human beings have an energy that can cause an interaction with other humans, even at a distance. It is a well-known fact that one person's energy can have a healthful/positive or unhealthful/negative effect on another merely by their presence.

A photographic system to capture the human energy field was developed by Semyon Kirlian in 1939. This system involved the photographing of subjects in the presence of a high-frequency, high-voltage, low-amperage electrical field and resulted in photos of human bodies enveloped in a luminous aura. It could even photograph a similar luminous energy field around fruits and vegetables and non-living things. In 1911, medical doctor Walter Kilner reported seeing human energy through coloured screens and filters. He described seeing a glowing mist around the whole body that appeared in three layers: a 6 mm dark layer closest to the skin surrounded by a 25 mm wide vaporous layer streaming perpendicularly from the body, and finally a delicate luminosity of around 15 cm in diameter. According to Kilner, auras differ from subject to subject depending on age, sex, mental ability and physical vitality. He was able to diagnose diseases via the variation and patches in a patient's aura.

Over a period of time many scientists, doctors, psychiatrists and healers have studied and experimented with human energy fields using electronic devices, medical instruments and even clairvoyance. By observing energy patterns they are able to make a diagnosis of any physical, physiological and mental ailments, thereby giving clear indications that the electromagnetic and light emissions from human bodies are closely related to the person's health.

One of the most significant works in this field had been carried out by Dr Valerie Hunt, who conducted research that demonstrated colour and frequency correlations. In a series of experiments recording frequency and wave patterns from different body parts, Dr Hunt and associates concluded that the auric colour bands correlate with the same frequency wave pattern as the chakras. Their research in February 1988 showed the following colour/frequency correlations (which are measured in hertz or Hz):

Colour	Frequency band (Hz)
Blue	250–275, plus 1200
Green	250–475
Yellow	500–700
Orange	950–1050
Red	1000–1200
Violet	1000–2000, plus 300–400, 600–800
White	1100–2000

Dr Hunt also stated that the chakras' frequencies follow exactly the same colour patterns mentioned in tantric and metaphysical literatures. She associated the chakras with these colours:

- **muladhara** (base root) with red
- **swadhisthana** (sacral) with orange
- **manipura** (solar plexus) with yellow
- **anahata** (heart) with green
- **vishuddhi** (throat) with blue
- **ajna** (third eye) with violet
- **sahasrara** (crown) with white.

Dr Hunt's research explains that the frequencies and colour patterns showing up in different chakras are the result of the physiological activity of the organs associated with the chakras. For example, our muladhara or base root chakra is associated with the organs of elimination, the gonads and the physical body, and their energy frequency shows up as the colour red in the auric field and so on. The activity in certain chakras sometimes triggers increased activity in another, which again proves that the chakras are both related and interdependent.

Dr Robert O. Becker, author of *The Body Electric*, documented human body energy in terms of electrical frequency. Bruce Tainio of

Tainio Technology in Cheney, Washington, the first person to measure the frequency of the human body and foods, developed a calibrated frequency monitor in 1992 to determine the relationship between frequency and disease. Measured in megahertz (MHz), he observed that a healthy body typically has a frequency ranging from 62 to 78 MHz and that when the frequency drops the immune system gets compromised. Below is a list of frequency vibrations:

Body part	Frequency (MHz)
Genius brain	80-8
Brain	72-90
Normal brain	72
Human body	62-78
Human body from the neck up	72-78
Human body from the neck down	60-68
Thyroid and parathyroid glands	62-68
Thymus gland	65-68
Heart	67-70
Lungs	58-65
Liver	55-60

Pancreas	60-80
Colds and flu	Begin at 57-60
Disease	Begins at 58
Candida overgrowth	Begins at 55
Receptive to Epstein Barr	52
Receptive to cancer	42
Death	Begins at 25

Source: https://bit.ly/1OpcYNX

Our energy vibrations can be affected by various factors, extrinsic and intrinsic both. The ***extrinsic*** or external factors that can affect our health and vibrations include the following.

Our dwelling unit. Ancient Hindu philosophy gives a lot of importance to balancing the energies of our dwelling unit. The traditional Hindu system of architecture known as vastu shastra provides guidelines for designing an energetically balanced dwelling unit before construction. Vastu shastra takes into account the four directions — east, west, north and south — and the movement of the sun and its energies in different directions before assigning different areas of the unit for the main entrance, kitchen, bedroom, toilets, prayer room and so on.

It is recommended that as many doors and windows as possible be positioned facing east or north-east, and that bodies of water be positioned in the north or north-east. Prayer rooms or temples should face north-east, called ishana, which is also the direction of Kubera, the lord of wealth. Today, the popular art of feng shui is useful to balance the energies of an already existing dwelling unit.

Geopathic stress. When there is an underground drain or river beneath a dwelling it has a draining effect on the energies of the residents and affects their health. Such locations should always be avoided when constructing a dwelling. These days there are all sorts of man-made energy stressors in urban areas such as mobile phone towers, concealed wiring and plumbing and household gadgets.

Polarity. According to vastu shastra our bodies are like magnets, since all fluids in the body are biomagnetic in nature. The head represents the North Pole and the feet represent the South Pole. It is common knowledge that similar magnetic poles repel energies; therefore it is recommended that a person should not sleep with the head towards north as this may cause a disturbance in the energy flow in the body, resulting in broken sleep and poor health.

Numbers. There are hidden numerical patterns that serve as keys for unlocking the secrets of the psyche. According to numerology, each number is associated with a particular planet, and planetary influences affect our life and also the chakras. For example, people having a birth or life path number of 1 are ruled by the sun, which strengthens the manipura (solar plexus) chakra and makes these people very ambitious in life. In the same way the number 2 is ruled by the moon, which influences the swadhisthana (sacral) chakra and in turn regulates our emotional balance. As a part of the numerical pattern, certain numbers resonate well with us and certain numbers do not; the science of numerology is based on this fact.

Geometry. In tantra practice, yantras are the tools used to balance energy and vibrations. Yantras are geometrical representations of cosmic energy that can be activated with mantras; they have the ability to create positive vibrations, and have a balancing effect on our own energies and of the energy of the area in which they are placed.

The *intrinsic* factors that can affect our health arise out of our lifestyles and lifestyle practices and include the following.

Physical/nutritional lifestyle. Physical lifestyle goes hand in hand with nutritional lifestyle. A healthy physical regimen is not only good for our physical bodies but also helps our mental and emotional beings. There is a lot of weight behind the maxim 'You are what you eat', as the food we eat ultimately becomes us. Ayurveda gives a lot of importance to food and nutrition, recommending a diet suitable to the particular body type as it believes that most diseases originate from our digestive system.

Mental and emotional lifestyles. These play a major role in affecting our health and vibrations: a single negative thought or emotional imbalance induced by stress, anxiety or depression can cause a dip in the energy levels of a person, up to 12 MHz, while an uplifting feeling such as enthusiasm or a positive outcome gives a positive charge and could raise the energy frequency by up to 10 MHz. Even spiritual practices such as prayer and meditation can increase energy levels by up to 15 MHz.

In chronic or acute depression and anxiety, negative thought processes can end up becoming an entrenched pattern, leading to a continuous drain on energy. Prolonged levels of stress, anxiety, depression or unease not only result in lowering body energy, they also affect our diet and assimilation of food, compromising our immune system and allowing the process of disease to set in. It has been observed that when energy starts dipping and goes down to 58 MHz or lower, our immune system starts giving in and the process of disease sets in, as in cases of all psychosomatic disorders. While modern health practitioners are still researching the association between mental emotional conditions and various ailments such as headaches/migraines, chronic aches and pains, menstrual imbalances, heart problems and so on, the understanding of the chakra system and its association with various organs and glands gives us insight into the effects of different mental and emotional stresses on our health and the process of disease.

Energy metabolism

To maintain and sustain the ideal vibrational level of 62-78 MHz, we supplement our physical energy through the foods we eat. Various foods provide us with energy in frequencies from 0-40 MHz. The lowest energy, 0-10 MHz, is from canned, refrigerated or preserved foods, which create lethargy in the body and are classified as tamasic (low-vibration/low-consciousness) food by Ayurveda. All modern foods, both vegetarian and non-vegetarian, provide energy in the range of 10-20 MHz. They may look good due to genetically modified fertilisers being fed to the plants but they don't have sufficient nutrients, which is why health-conscious people seek organic or eco-harvested food products — which offer up to 30 MHz of energy. The highest food energy of up to 40 MHz comes from living food such as sprouts.

Whether we bow down to our taste buds or choose our food consciously, once the food is tasted, chewed and swallowed we don't have any control over it: how much nutrients we draw from the food we eat and how much of those nutrients will go to which organs of the body is not within our control. This process is driven by our body's intelligence or the autonomous nervous system, which ensures that the vital organs of the body are provided with nutrients first. From the chakra perspective the manipura (solar plexus) chakra is responsible for digestion and assimilation. The energy associated with this chakra is called samana vayu; 'samana' in Hindi is 'balance', so this is the energy of balance and is responsible for the balanced distribution of nutrients to different organs according to their requirements.

When we are not healthy physically, mentally or emotionally we either do not eat well or absorb nutrients well. In either case, a deficiency or lack of nutrients is then passed on to the skin and hair. It is important for our survival that the vital organs get their required amount of nutrients. When there is a deficiency the body's intelligence cuts it from the skin, the largest organ of the body; however, the health of the skin doesn't threaten our survival. Skin can always recover and become better when a person regains health. Therefore the maxim that 'skin is the mirror of health' is indeed true. When we are not healthy physically, mentally or emotionally it is reflected in the quality of the skin. Dull-looking skin, dark circles under the eyes, hair loss and other skin conditions such as eczema or psoriasis indicate an underlying health condition and the stress levels of the person.

Energy can be neither created nor destroyed. The food we consume is converted to energy and is used to sustain the vital organs of the body. Each organ requires a minimum amount of energy to work at its optimal level and to then release processed energy out of the body. This processed energy moves through the nadis (the channels of energy) and converges at the chakras to be released from the body. The processed energy released from the body forms a spiral, like a tornado on the surface of Earth, and envelops the physical body. This is what shows up as the energetic layer in our subtle body.

The seven layers of the human energy field

Chakras are energy vortices, points of exchange between individual and universal energy. The energy vibrations released from various chakras envelop the physical body, forming a layer around it, known as our subtle or energy body. These energy vibrations from each chakra have varying frequencies depending on the energy metabolism of individual organs, hence they appear to form distinct layers. The seven chakra vibrations resonate with the vibrations of the seven colours, like a rainbow.

- The first layer of the energy, closest to our physical body, is associated with the muladhara (base root) chakra and is known as our etheric body. It shows up as red in the energy field.

- The second layer is associated with the swadhisthana (sacral) chakra and is known as our emotional body. It shows up as orange in the energy field.

- The third layer is associated with the manipura (solar plexus) chakra and is known as our mental body. It shows up as yellow in the energy field.

- The fourth layer of energy is associated with the anahata (heart) chakra and is known as our astral body. It shows up as green in the energy field.

- The fifth layer is associated with the vishuddhi (throat) chakra and is known as our etheric template body. It shows up as blue in the energy field.

- The sixth layer is associated with the ajna (third eye) chakra and is known as our celestial body. It shows up as indigo in the energy field.

- These layers are all enveloped with the seventh layer, which is associated with the sahasrara (crown) chakra and is known as our causal or ketheric body. It shows up as violet, white or gold in ascended masters.

The chakra/colour vibrations are not distinct layers, but are intermingled in the energy field. When an aura picture is taken, the colour dominant in the aura represents the dominant chakra at that moment. The seven energetic layers together with the skeletal system and the skin make up a total of nine layers. At the time of death the soul leaves the physical body along with all of the energy layers.

3

Tantra

'Kundalini is the biological basis of . . . genius.'
— Gopi Krishna

There are many misconceptions about just what tantra is. It is not about sensory gratifications or sex, nor it is a religion or a cult; it is a philosophy. The word 'tantra' comprises two words: tanoti, meaning 'expansion'; and trayati, meaning 'liberation'. Ayurveda and yoga are part of tantric philosophy, working together hand in hand and laying down a complete system of practical understanding of human beings. The chakra system is a part of the same philosophy. Tantric practices incorporate yoga, breath work, yantras and mantras.

According to tantra, the range of our mental experiences can be broadened with the help of the senses. Our mind can have an experience of an object within the framework of time and space, or even beyond the framework of time, space and object when the mind expands beyond its defined boundaries. There is a release of energy and a shift in consciousness. This latent energy within all of us is described as our kundalini in tantra and yoga.

From the beginning of creation mankind has witnessed many transcendental happenings: child geniuses, people with various supernatural, psychic or intuitive abilities, able to read minds, make true predictions or perform miracle healing. We all have different capabilities: the ability to write highly inspiring poems, to create beautiful music or paintings, or an incredible intellect. Humankind came to understand that within every individual there is a special form of energy that is dormant in most, evolving in some and fully awakened in a few. This energy was originally named after gods and goddesses, angels and the divine, while some called it prana shakti, or rising consciousness.

Ancient sages, yogis and tantrics recognised this dynamic force in human bodies and termed it *kundalini shakti,* the essential conscious power responsible for human development and all life functions. It is also manifested in personal development, non-ordinary states and spiritual transformation.

The yogi Gopi Krishna described kundalini as being a biological mechanism present in every human being. According to him, the human cerebrospinal system is capable of an amazing activity that is yet to be defined by science and can be accelerated through the disciplines of yoga and meditation or by certain spiritual practices. The correct practice of meditation carried on regularly for a sufficient duration of time tends to force a normally silent region in the brain to an astonishing activity; in a state of meditation a person connects with universal energies and is able to receive cosmic vibrations. Tantra explains how under the direct influence of the cosmic energies our brains, which are still in a state of organic evolution, are able to expand psychic abilities.

Kundalini yoga considers the physical body to be a vessel filled with consciousness. It considers that supreme consciousness represents the highest possible manifestation of physical matter in this body. A kundalini experience, considered from the viewpoint of individual transformation, is said to be the path to enlightenment. The matter of the physical body is transformed into subtle forces such as feeling, thinking, reasoning, remembering, postulating and doubting. In this gradual process of evolution the psyche — suprasensory or transcendental power — is the ultimate point in human evolution.

In spite of its conscious awakening, sometimes kundalini remains in one of the higher chakras for many years or lifetimes. This blockage at a particular chakra may sometimes result in a person realising certain psychic powers (siddhis) associated with that chakra. Instead of understanding that they are on a path of spiritual growth and need to work further to clear karmic blocks for further ascension, sometimes the sadhaka (spiritual practitioner) will start displaying this psychic power, thus nurturing their ego and hindering their further spiritual journey.

The awakening of kundalini and its ascension process through the chakras is important for the evolution of mankind, as our present state of mind is not capable of handling all of the aspects of life. The essence of our relationships with people, the love and the hatred, is formed by our mental states. Our agonies, pains and frustrations are not due to life circumstances but more to our mental conditioning, temperaments and responses to life situations.

In his *Yoga Sutras*, Patanjali mentioned that all pains and sufferings arise out of the modification of mind and from attachments to people and things. Possessiveness, jealousy and self-centredness are traits that arise when consciousness gets stuck in the mundane. During the process of the awakening of kundalini the mind is automatically stabilised and our perception of the world changes. Though the world remains the same the changed perception leads to a change of values in life, improving the quality of love and relationships and enabling us to balance out the disappointments and frustrations.

Kundalini awakening is the awakening of consciousness. Kundalini shakti travels through sushumna nadi, activating all of the chakras on its way up, to become one with higher consciousness at the sahasrara (crown) chakra. At that time the entire store of energy in man is unleashed, activating the higher centres in the brain and enabling us to attain enlightenment. During this process, the energy, which can be used to heal, transform and energise, evolves into higher awareness.

There is a great deal of mysticism around the concept of kundalini, and anybody who knows even a little about it wants their kundalini to be awakened; if a large number of enlightened people were to appear in society it would result in a transformation. Kundalini awakening cannot be the sole objective of any spiritual practice; in fact, it is the by-product of all spiritual practices, yoga or meditation and also our karma. It will happen only when we are destined for it.

Gunas

The word 'kundalini' comes from the Sanskrit word 'kundal', meaning a coil, and is represented by a serpent coiled three and a half times and with its tail in its mouth. The comparison of a serpent with kundalini comes from the nature of its movement, which is spiralling and serpent-like. The three full coils represent the three gunas or the three states of consciousness: waking, sleeping and dreaming. These relate to the three types of experience: subjective, sensual (objective) and no experience. The half-coiled tail in the serpent's mouth represents the ego.

According to tantric and Ayurvedic texts the human body is composed of five elements: earth, water, fire, air and ether. An Ayurvedic practitioner assesses the combination of these five elements, and according to the dominance of certain elements categorises the body types into one of three doshas: vatta, pitta and kapha. This is done mainly from a health perspective so that diet, exercise and even medication can be prescribed to correct the imbalances. From a spiritual perspective, tantra describes the combination of the five elements into three levels of consciousness, called gunas: tamas, rajas and sattva. Our consciousness evolves from the lower to the higher chakras, from gross to subtle or from tamas to sattva.

Tamas	Darkness, inertia, inactivity, materiality
Rajas	Energy, action, change, movement
Sattva	Harmony balance, joy, intelligence

Tamas obscures truth behind illusion. Associated with the muladhara (base root) chakra, it is the lowest level of consciousness, where a human is trying to evolve from animal consciousness just to fulfil the needs of the physical body without discrimination. It represents grossness, inertia, darkness, dullness and resistance.

Rajas embodies the principle of activity, representing energy, movement of consciousness, turbulence, power and desire. Rajas is activity at the conscious level, and involves movement from muladhara to manipura via swadhisthana; it activates the desire centres of the body, causing manifestations.

Sattva, a higher level of consciousness, is light in nature. It is the principle of sublimation, representing light, truth, perception, intelligence and harmony. When kundalini moves from manipura to anahata and upwards we become conscious of our words and actions, and let go of greed and attachments. This shift of consciousness leads to spiritual awakening.

Tamas and sattva are two opposites of the same coin. In both a person abandons the world of senses: evolving and merging into light in sattva, and going down and merging into darkness in tamas.

The gunas can be compared to the three states of matter: solid, liquid and gaseous. Water as an element serves as the best example, as it exists in all three forms:

- In its solid state as ice it represents grossness, inertia and immobility, which is described as being 'tamasic'. When our consciousness is in tamas it is engrossed with fulfilling the needs of the physical body.

- When solid ice starts melting and flowing it is active, or 'rajasic'; this is when we start developing a certain amount of discrimination and evolve to fulfil our needs with the rightful means.

47

- With a further rise in heat water starts evaporating into steam, leaving all the impurities behind. This is a process of sublimation where conscious energy becomes pure, and is called sattva. In this state we experience a transformation of consciousness, move beyond greed and ego, feel detached from people and material things and seek a life of truth.

Each of the three gunas is present in us, never becoming separated from each other; when one guna dominates the other two become recessive. Like a three-coloured strand braided together, at one time one colour appears most dominant on the surface and at other times other colours are more visible. All three are always present, but sometimes one overlaps and hides the others from view. When sattva dominates, rajas and tamas are pushed into background; at that time all desires, attachments, confusion and ignorance disappear, and all that remains is light and bliss. When rajas dominates there is a great rush of energy and a strong will to undertake work, projects and activities. When tamas dominates it makes a person self-centred and focused on fulfilling their own needs by whatever means they can. They also try to impose their whims, fancies and ideas on other people. Only when they start thinking beyond themselves for their fellow beings, keeping the greater good of society in mind, will their consciousness starts evolving.

As long as we are embodied all three gunas are necessary, as they are interdependent and help each other in the process of evolution and self-development. In the process of bringing each other out, one guna serves as the stepping stone for another: a thing that is stable and tamas-dominated is provided motivation and activity by rajas, and that motion and activity help in the process of realisation. Ultimately, we move to attain our true and essential nature, which is light or sattva.

The natural flow of evolution is from subtle to gross. Ideas exist, first in a person's mind and then followed by activity, which will initiate a downward flow of energy. This downward flow continues until the energy gets entrapped in gross form. From sattva to rajas to tamas, this is the natural course of evolution, although rajas can also be used to convert tamas back into sattva. With the five sense organs and five organs of action — feet/locomotion, hands/dexterity, rectum/excretion, genitals/reproduction, mouth/speech — a person has the choice to either flow with gravity downwards to tamas or rise through activity upwards into sattva and light.

The five elements

Ayurveda believes that we are the microcosm of the macrocosm, that everything that exists outside the physical body — flora, fauna, minerals and metals — also exists inside. The body, which has its oneness with the universe, is composed of five elements (panch mahabhoot): earth, water, fire, air and ether (or space). All of the five elements have psychological correspondences that indicate the state of mind and the qualities of emotions. Each of the five elements is associated with our lower five chakras, as the lower chakras are important for the physical plane of existence. The five elements represent the finer qualities of matter: solid, liquid, radiant, gaseous and ethereal. They delineate the five densities of all substances, all visible or invisible matter in the universe.

The three gunas are also associated with the five elements. Sattva, consisting of clarity, is associated with ether; rajas, consisting of energy, with fire; and tamas, consisting of inertia, with earth. Between sattva and rajas flows the subtle but mobile element of air, and between rajas and tamas flows the element of water, combining mobility and inertia.

The five elements constitute a continuum of energy, from its densest and grossest vibrational level to the most subtle. At its lowest level vibrational energy has substance (solidity), whereby atoms are compactly packed and cohesively formed; that's why it's called dense and gross. This lowest level is the earth element. When excited to a higher frequency the earth element loses its solidity; the energy is less dense as the atoms are more dispersed and free flowing. With a higher frequency the substance becomes fluid and is called the water element. At this level the molecules of the fluid still retain cohesiveness and form, although the form is that of the vessel holding the fluid.

As the level of vibrations keep increasing, heat and light are generated by the accelerated motion; in this state the matter is less cohesive. Energy in this form is quite radiant and is represented by the fire element. As the speed of individual particles continues to accelerate all form is lost, heat and light are no longer produced and any cohesiveness of the matter is dissipated. It is now represented by air.

Finally, when the matter has lost all tactile qualities and is perceptible to humans only as sound, it has attained the most subtle vibration and is represented by ether. In this state the individual particles of the matter no longer exist, but have rather vibrated beyond the material plane.

Our physical or gross body represents the earth element, as Mother Earth is a balance of minerals and metals in the same way our physical bodies contain a balance of mineral and metals. Any imbalance of these minerals and metals affects our health at the physical level. The source of minerals and metals in the physical body is the food we eat, irrespective of whether it is vegetarian or non-vegetarian. The muladhara (base root) chakra is responsible for the gross/physical body, hence the earth element is attributed to this chakra.

The universe is two-thirds water, in the same way two-thirds of our bodies are composed of fluids represented by blood, lymph, saliva and so on. We are aware and it is also visible to us that the lunar cycles or moon phases affect the water on Earth, causing high tides and low tides; in the same way, moon phases affect the water in our body, although it is not visible but it can be felt as emotional imbalance in sensitive people, especially the water signs. Therefore, the swadhisthana (sacral) chakra is responsible for our emotional balance and is associated with our emotional body.

The manipura (solar plexus) chakra is associated with the element of fire. Our bodies contain the energy of fire in three forms: body temperature, which fluctuates in a narrow range, mental energy (bhoot agni) and digestive fire (jathar agni). Solar energy also nourishes our body's fire element with vitamin D.

Our breath represents the air element, with each breath providing us with vital oxygen and sustaining us with vital pranas. This element is associated with the anahata (heart) chakra.

Ether is considered to be the most vital of the five elements, as without space no movement or circulation is possible. Without circulation everything will become so gross that life simply cannot exist. This element is associated with the vishuddhi (throat) chakra.

The importance of the five elements in our lives can also be recognised through the fact that our physical bodies can survive without food (which nourishes the earth element) for about 21 to 30 days and without water for seven to 10 days. If our body temperature moves beyond or below the normal range of temperature we can survive for only a few hours. Air sustains life; without air we can survive only for a few minutes. This body of ours is a potential space. Our blood, lymph, breath, food and everything in the body moves because there is space inside; without the space we will just be dead. When a person dies all the energies leave the physical body along with the space, which is why bodies turns rigid. Ayurveda insists on the balance of the five elements as the foundation of good health.

Nadis

Our bodies have four main systems of distributing prana:

- **The circulatory system:** comprising arteries, veins and lymphatic systems.

- **The nervous system:** including the central, sympathetic and parasympathetic nervous systems.

- **The endocrine system:** comprising various ductless glands that regulate body physiology and various aspects and functionings of the physical body through the secretion of hormones.

- **The nadis:** the conduits of energy in the subtle body.

The subtle body consists of a channel system of energy known as nadis. The word 'nadi' originates from the Sanskrit word *nad*, meaning 'movement'. According to Rig Veda (sacred text) it also means 'stream', although the literal meaning of nadi is 'flow'. As part of the circulatory system the physical body has various streams such as arteries, veins and lymphatic vessels; these are channels for the flow of consciousness. As both negative and positive energy flow into the body through a complex circuit like meridians, similarly consciousness flows into the body through nadis. The ego or ahamkara does not reside in the physical body but in the subtle body, and moves in the nadis. When awakened the dormant energy of kundalini also works through the nadis.

According to tantric texts, there are 72,000 nadis (channels) in our body that are the conduits of pranas. Of these numerous nadis, 10 are significant and three of those 10 are the most significant; they form the basis of kundalini tantra. These three nadis are:

- **ida** (left or lunar nadi), representing the cooling energy of the moon
- **pingala** (right or solar nadi), representing the heating energy of the sun; and
- **sushumna**, which is closely associated with the spine and spinal cord at the subtle level. Sushumna runs through the centre of the energetic spine and corresponds to the spinal canal; chakras are strung upon it like lotuses.

Sushumna, considered to be the most important of all of the nadis, starts at the muladhara (base root) chakra and culminates at the sahasrara (crown) chakra.

From a numerological perspective $7 + 2 + 0 + 0 + 0$ adds up to 9, which in a spiritual sense is considered to be the number of completion. This is why mala or prayer beads have 108 or 54 beads, both of which add up to 9. Our physical body has nine openings or doorways through which we experience the world, and the pranas can enter or leave the physical body from these doorways. The nine body openings are associated with our sense organs: two eyes, two nostrils, two ears, the mouth, the anus and the genitals. Most of the nadis begin or terminate at these openings.

Control of the nadis enables us in turn to control the ego, the mind and the senses, as the pranas moving with the breath kindle the body's fire and are carried to the mind.

Nadis move in the body through each and every part, being the subtle counterpart of the physical flow of nervous energy and blood. They are not described in terms of structures but rather as conduits or channels. Ida represents conscious energy and knowing, while pingala is vital and life-giving; they are roughly translated as mind and body. As we discuss the polarisation of the individual, mind and body themselves are polarised but complementary to each other. Ida represents the moon's energy and pingala the energy of the sun.

Sushumna, representing the spirit or consciousness, is supreme and is the channel for kundalini shakti.

The ancient discipline of swar yoga (the yoga of breath) states that our temperament and nature change according to the dominance of our breathing nostrils. At any given time our breath does not come in equal volume through both nostrils, except for a brief period. Most of the time one nostril is more active and dominant than other one, and this dominance alternates between left and right nostrils in a regular pattern.

The left nostril is associated with the ida nadi, which connects with the right hemisphere of the brain, while the right nostril is associated with pingala nadi, which connects to the left hemisphere of the brain. The movement of energy through these nadis, from one hemisphere to the other, happens simultaneously with the change of breath from one nostril to the other. Therefore, when the right nostril dominates pingala is active and the left hemisphere dominates. When the left nostril dominates ida is active and the right hemisphere dominates. When both nostrils operate evenly both hemispheres operate in unison.

When energy concentrates in the left hemisphere, solar energy is drawn by the right nostril and a person becomes more active, verbal, intellectual, extroverted, ambitious, creative and masculine. Conversely, when the right hemisphere dominates it draws on lunar energy through the left nostril, and a person is characterised by femininity, passivity, introversion, emotional responses and orientation to sight and sound.

The three nadis — ida, pingala and sushumna — start from the muladhara chakra at the pelvic floor. From here sushumna flows directly upwards within the central canal to the sahasrara chakra, while ida passes to the left and pingala to the right, crisscrossing each other at each higher chakra.

Sushumna flows inside the central canal of the spinal cord, while ida and pingala flow simultaneously on the outer surface of the spinal cord but still within the bony vertebral column. In human physiology, these two nadis roughly correspond with the two halves of the autonomous nervous system: the sympathetic and the parasympathetic. Pingala coincides with the sympathetic nerves, which are responsible for stimulation and the acceleration of activities; it tends to utilise a lot of internal energy. The sympathetic nerves speed up the heart, dilate the blood vessels, increase the respiration rate and intensify the efficiency of the eyes and ears and so on.

The parasympathetic nerves directly oppose the sympathetic nerves as they reduce the heartbeat, constrict the blood vessels and slow the breathing rate so that a person becomes an introvert. The flow of prana in ida and pingala is completely involuntary. Basically, the pingala nadi represents the components of action and controls all of the vital processes, while the ida nadi represents reception and controls all of the mental processes.

Ida can be viewed as the energy within the personality, which is passive, receptive, feminine, negative and yin. At the physical level, it is dark, cold, lunar, energy-dissipating, entropic, expansive (centrifugal) and relaxing. It is emotional, feeling, intuitive and non-discriminative, which is also the soma-psychic aspect of a person where energy is inwardly directed and the body acts on the mind. Ida controls the feeling centres and sense organs (gyanendriyas), thereby giving us awareness and knowledge of the world in which we live.

Pingala can be defined as masculine, dynamic, active, positive, yang energy within our personalities. It has a physical and mental side, representing light, heat, solar energy, creativity, organisation, focus (centripetal) and contractive. It is psychosomatic energy, and directs the organs of action (karmendriyas) outwards. It is the basic life-giving energy.

Our body chemistry, which is reflected in our feelings and temperament, can be altered easily by changing the breath pattern. One of our gurus used to say that the entire world population could be divided into two categories of people: one dominant in the left nostril and the other dominant in the right nostril. Where the left nostril is dominant the ida nadi is overactive and draws in more lunar energy, which in turn makes people more emotional by nature. These people are creative, moody and prone to depression; they are also prone to having a low body temperature and low blood pressure.

When the right nostril is dominant the pingala nadi is overactive, which affects the manipura (solar plexus) chakra. These people draw in more solar energy and are driven, making them very ambitious in life. They push themselves and others around them to fulfil their life ambitions, chasing money, power or authority. They tend to be multi-taskers, as their minds are always busy planning too many things at one time. These people are sometimes not grounded and lose focus on the activity at hand. They tend to have a high body temperature, may have a heated liver and are prone to hypertension, high blood pressure, high blood sugar/diabetes, headaches and migraines.

Yoga and tantra have gone hand in hand to devise exercises to restore the balance of energies to promote wellness. The imbalance of the ida and pingala nadis can be restored by practising breathing through alternate nostrils (anulom vilom). The practices of kundalini yoga are focused on the awakening of sushumna; once sushumna comes to life a means of communication between the higher and lower centres of consciousness is established, which leads to the awakening of kundalini.

Granthis

Tantric scriptures talk about three granthis or psychic knots in the physical body. These granthis represent the three fundamental principles of energy: creation, sustenance and dissolution. As mentioned previously, ida, pingala and sushumna rise from muladhara at the pelvic floor; sushumna flows directly upwards within the central canal, while ida passes to the left and pingala passes to the right, crisscrossing at each of the higher chakras. Located at the points of crossing over are the three granthis.

The granthis, which are basically levels of awareness, are named after the three Hindu deities forming the trinity: Brahma (the energy of creation), Vishnu (the energy of sustenance) and Rudra (or Shiva, the energy of dissolution). Granthis pose as obstacles or barriers, and on the path of raising the consciousness each aspirant has to cross the barriers. During the process of kundalini movement and spiritual progress our consciousness moves through the granthis.

The **brahma granthi** is located in the region of muladhara, exactly at the T junction of the muladhara (base root) and swadhisthana (sacral) chakras. It is the first crossover point in the path of kundalini awakening. Some tantric scriptures place the brahma granthi in the region of the navel, as it is also considered to be the knot of samsara (the world of names and forms). Muladhara is associated with the physical body, with our attachment to material things, physical pleasures and self-centredness — the world of maya, or illusion. According to Hinduism, the deity Brahma is the creator of the universe, so the energy of procreation is also associated with this granthi; unless this psychic knot is open in both the partners a couple will not be able to conceive a child, which may explain why some couples are unable to have children despite having everything right biologically.

The brahma granthi is the major obstacle in the spiritual path, creating a lot of restlessness and distraction of the mind. Until the time our consciousness stays embedded in tamas (the mundane or gross world) our mind is trapped; we are ignorant of reality, living in the world of senses or experiencing lethargy and negativity and acting egocentrically. To overcome the obstacles associated with brahma granthi an aspirant has to go beyond the senses and sensory pleasures, and rise beyond tamas. Once the energy becomes pure and radiant this knot can be untied, which frees the aspirant from the bondages of attachments and selfishness.

The **vishnu granthi** is located at the crossover point of the anahata (heart) chakra. It is associated with bondages created by attachments, especially emotional attachments to people and things. In his Yoga Sutras Patanjali mentioned attachments as being the main source of pain and suffering. Anahata is mainly associated with devotion, love and faith; however, our emotional attachments are the main cause of heart chakra imbalances. When we promote detachment, it doesn't mean you do not care for the other person. Consider the difference between empathy and sympathy. Empathy is a balanced state where you can understand someone's pain or suffering while maintaining your own balance. Sympathy is an imbalance arising from attachment, where we actually feel someone's pain or suffering and lose our balance also. These attachments are hindrances to spiritual progress; only through detachment or vivek (absolute discrimination), knowledge and faith can we untie this psychic knot.

In ancient India, a spiritual aspirant would forgo family life (grihastha ashram) and undertake asceticism (sannyasa ashram) by giving up worldly ties and home life, thereby freeing themselves from the deep ties of attachment with the family. Such people are known as 'divij' (twice born) and live for their spiritual aspirations only. This is still practised by some seekers in the Jain religion of India.

The **rudra granthi** is located in the area of the ajna (third eye) chakra. Rudra is another name of Lord Shiva when he is referred to as the lord of dissolution. The untying of this psychic knot leads to the end of duality and results in the dissolution of an aspirant's ego. This granthi is also associated with attachment to siddhis (psychic powers), which may nurture the ego and cause a hindrance in spiritual progress. Unless the seeker is willing to surrender the ego, further spiritual progress will not happen. Hence this granthi is the point of transcendence wherein time-bound consciousness gets dissolved and a yogi is established into infinity by ascending to the crown chakra and experiences a state of bliss.

Vayus

The human body has two types of nervous system: sympathetic (sensory or information) and parasympathetic (motor). According to tantra, we have two types of energy reaching every organ of the body: vital/ dynamic (prana shakti) energy and mental (manas shakti) energy. The vital energy, prana, flows in the body through the nadis, the conduits of energy. Nerves are part of the physical body, while the nadis are part of the subtle body.

We describe chakras as the energy centres of the body; however, the energy at each chakra has a different role. In a tantric context each chakra's energy is called vayu, though the literal meaning of the word is 'wind'. This vital energy has five variants that are responsible for different functions in the body:

■ **Prana vayu:** when we talk of prana, we are talking about the vital life-giving energy, not just the breath, air or oxygen. This prana energy is located in the area of the larynx at the top of the diaphragm and is associated with the heart chakra. It is responsible for our survival and governs all the functions of the heart and lungs, along with other activities in the region of the heart chakra including breathing, swallowing and blood circulation.

■ **Apana vayu:** centred in the pelvic region between the navel and the perineum, this energy is associated with the muladhara (base root) chakra. We receive cosmic vibrations and vital pranas through the sahasrara (crown) chakra. These pranas circulate and feed our bodies, and the processed pranas are then eliminated through the root chakra. Apana vayu has a downward flow, regulating all the elimination processes in the body; it is responsible for the expulsion of gas, wind, faeces, urine and even foetuses at the time of birth.

■ **Vyana vayu:** associated with the swadhisthana (sacral) chakra, this vital force pervades the whole body and governs the circulatory system. It regulates the movement of all fluids including blood, lymph, saliva and menstrual fluid. Emotional blockages affect our swadhisthana chakra and affect the movement of this energy. This in turn affects the movement of fluids and particularly lymphatic fluids, which may also cause physical or physiological complications in the body that affect the reproductive organs and glands, causing lymphatic congestion and fluid retention.

■ **Samana vayu:** 'samana' means 'equal' or 'balanced'. This energy is centred in the small intestine between the navel and ribcage, and provides balance between the two opposite energies of apana and prana vayu. Associated with the manipura (solar plexus) chakra, it is here that food is digested, assimilated and converted into nutrition. This energy activates and controls the digestive organs and their secretions and ensures a balanced distribution of nutrients to each organ, especially vital organs, according to their needs.

■ **Udana vayu:** 'udana' means 'flight', as our spoken words fly away from us. Centred in the throat, this energy controls the sympathetic and parasympathetic nervous systems and communication of all kinds: our will, memory and even exhalation. Blockages of this energy affect the functioning of the vishuddhi (throat) chakra and may cause issues related to the thyroid.

The senses

Our awareness within this body constitutes the waking state of consciousness, which is made up of 16 components: five sensory organs, five organs of action, five elements and the mind. The energetic basis or pure form of the physical body is the subtle body; the subtle body is also composed of 16 components. Within the subtle body exist the seven major chakras, which have an association with the five senses of smell, taste, sight, touch and hearing.

Smell. Our sense of smell is primordial, the most basic sense. It is associated with the muladhara chakra, wherein we evolve from animal consciousness to human consciousness. This is the most developed sense in animals and the one whereby they recognise their food, mate and medicine. A newborn baby recognises their mother only from the smell. It is also believed that out of the five senses this is the only one that transcends from this life to the next life, which is why we use flowers or incenses to please departed souls.

 Taste. The Indian name for the sacral chakra, swadhisthana, is composed of *swad*, meaning 'taste', and *sthan*, meaning 'place' or 'centre', so the sense of taste belongs to the sacral chakra. This chakra is the desire centre of our physical bodies, not only sexual desire but material and all other kinds. When the sacral chakra is imbalanced we are stuck in our desires, and when our desires are uncontrollable they lead to addictions. All addictions are the result of an imbalanced sacral chakra.

 Sight. The sense of sight is associated with the solar plexus chakra, as our optic nerve is under the influence of manipura. Mental stress or poor digestion, both of which are related to the solar plexus chakra, lead to headaches and migraines and indicate an imbalance in the chakra. Even anger, the seat of which is the solar plexus chakra, is visible in our eyes; suppressed anger shows up as a heated liver. When people develop diabetes or glaucoma their eyesight is affected, which is again under the influence of the solar plexus chakra.

Touch. We express our love through hugging or holding, touch being a therapy in itself. The anahata (heart) chakra is the one associated with love and is also the seat of the healer. We hold someone when we want to console them, and a loving couple can express their love of each other by holding hands, with no words required.

Hearing. The vishuddhi (throat) chakra is associated with our sense of hearing: we speak or express ourselves to be heard. When we are not able to express our emotions easily it results in blockages of the throat chakra. When the throat chakra is blocked for a prolonged period it affects our ears and sense of hearing, resulting in frequent ear problems, earaches, ear infections or ringing of the ears (tinnitus).

The sixth sense: intuition. We all have a certain sense of intuition, which is connected to our ajna (third eye) chakra. When this sense develops further along with spiritual growth and with a shift in consciousness we develop clairvoyance.

 The seventh sense: common sense. Common sense requires awareness. There are two things we do regularly but are not aware of. The first one is breathing. We all start breathing from the moment we come into the material world, but we are not conscious of it. One part of yoga is pranayama, which is completely devoted to breathing. According to tantra and yoga, our lives are not measured in the number of days, months or years but in the number of breaths assigned to each one of us; if we breathe fast we die young. Fast breathing is shallow breathing, which doesn't fill our lungs with oxygen and ultimately shows in the body and its health.

The second thing we do unconsciously is rubbing the body, which we all do almost every day when we bathe or shower. If we rub the body with awareness it will lead to good health. God has made our body very intelligently, with all our lymph nodes in the front of the body; we can rub those areas easily. The only lymph nodes that are towards the back are behind the knees and in the neck, called occipital nodes, and our hands can reach those. If we can focus on our lymph nodes when rubbing our bodies and keep them unblocked and healthy, most health issues such as niggling aches and pains, fluid retention and so on can be avoided.

4

Nervous and endocrine systems

The chakras represent the activity of our organs and glands: they are the barometers of our health. Yogic and spiritual practices impact the nerve plexuses and thus the chakras. Many people of scientific and yogic mind have sought to understand and explain the physical and psychic aspects of kundalini and the chakras; in particular Dr J.K. Sarkar, who in his paper 'Anatomical and Physiological Basis of Raja Yoga' tried to explain the working of chakras through the nervous and endocrine systems.

The human nervous system is composed of two parts: the central (or somatic) nervous system (CNS), which is responsible for voluntary actions, and the autonomic nervous system (ANS), which is independent of our will.

The CNS involves the brain and all its divisions within the skull, including the cerebral cortex, thalamus, hypothalamus, pituitary, pineal body, mid-brain, cerebellum, pons and medulla oblongata and the whole length of the spinal column. The CNS sends and receives nerve impulses to and from the entire body and its periphery with the help of 43 pairs of nerves arising from the brain and spinal cord. The higher centres for thinking, hearing, seeing, movement and so on are located in the different areas of the cerebral cortex. The four ventricles or cavities of the brain and the narrow canal in the spinal cord contain a fluid called cerebrospinal fluid, which flows in a continuous stream.

The ANS controls the activities of the internal organs and consists of two divisions: sympathetic and parasympathetic. Parasympathetic nerves arise from the brain and from the lower part of the spinal cord. Their actions are usually localised, such as slowing of the heart rate, and help to conserve body energy. The sympathetic system consists of nerves arising from the middle part of the spinal cord, forming two long trunks on the two sides of the spine and extending from the base of the skull to the coccyx.

The two sympathetic trunks contain several ganglions (congregation of nerve cells) that meet terminally at a small ganglion called the ganglion impar, which is located in front of the coccyx. Sympathetic nerves arising from the ganglia on these two trunks form various nerve plexuses (networks of fine nerves) on their way to different body organs such as the uterus, intestine and heart. The reactions of sympathetic nerves are mass reactions such as a constriction of arteries, acceleration of heart rate and slowing of gastric movement.

Sushumna is the central canal of the spinal cord; it continues into the cavities of the brain and is in direct contact with the hypothalamus and pineal gland. The spinal cord lies only in the upper two-thirds of the vertebral column. In the lower third of the spine it tapers off abruptly into a conical extremity. From the apex to this conical extremity a delicate non-nervous filament called the filum terminale descends to the coccyx, the lowest bone of the vertebral column. The lower part of the filum terminale is in the vicinity of the inferior hypogastric plexus. There are various other autonomic nerve plexuses situated on the two sides of the vertebral column; these are the lotuses associated with our chakras. The suggested anatomical sites for the chakra lotuses are as follows:

- **muladhara** (base root) chakra: inferior hypogastric (pelvic) plexus
- **swadhisthana** (sacral) chakra: superior hypogastric plexus
- **manipura** (solar plexus) chakra: coeliac or solar plexus

- **anahata** (heart) chakra: cardiac plexus
- **vishuddhi** (throat) chakra: plexuses connecting the superior, middle and inferior cervical ganglia
- **ajna** (third eye) chakra: internal carotid plexus
- **sahasrara** (crown) chakra: pineal body.

Glands of the endocrine system

The holistic approach to health fully acknowledges the integration of mind and body; the well-being of one depends on the good health of the other. Human bodies consist of two kinds of glands: exocrine and endocrine. Exocrine glands are the glands that release their secretions through ducts such as the liver and gall bladder. Endocrine glands do not have ducts and release their secretions, known as hormones, directly into the bloodstream. These glands are responsible for our bodies' physiological functioning. The hormones secreted by the endocrine glands are chemical messengers, and together with the autonomic nervous system they maintain the parameters for optimum growth. Since the nervous and endocrine systems are interconnected, then functionally an imbalance in one will affect the other.

Each of the seven main chakras is associated with a particular endocrine gland. Chakra health is affected by the functioning of the endocrine glands and vice versa: any imbalance in the chakras may affect the associated endocrine gland, manifesting in terms of physical or physiological symptoms.

The hypothalamus gland

The hypothalamus gland is a small region of the brain that activates and regulates that part of the nervous system responsible for controlling involuntary body functions, the hormonal system and many other body functions such as sleep regulation, body temperature and appetite. With complex interconnections with the cerebral cortex and the other parts of the brain that are little understood, it links emotions with the body's autonomic nervous system. It is regulated by the ajna (third eye) chakra.

The pituitary gland

The pituitary gland is a pea-sized structure that looks like an upside-down mushroom; it hangs by a stalk from the undersurface of the brain. This vital gland influences growth and metabolism and stimulates the activities of other glands. It orchestrates the secretion of hormones from other endocrine glands by producing a range of controller hormones such as human growth hormone, follicle-stimulating hormone, prolactin and thyroid-stimulating hormones (vasopressin and oxytocin). The hypothalamus gland controls the pituitary gland and indirectly masterminds its orchestration.

The pituitary gland has two lobes — anterior and posterior — that release a wide range of different hormones, including those responsible for contractions during childbirth and those that regulate the release of breast milk by a nursing mother. It is interesting to note that the intuition of a mother is at its peak while nursing. The process of nursing and intuition are also associated with the third eye chakra.

Adrenal glands

The adrenal glands are attached to the top of each kidney. They are associated with the muladhara (base root) chakra. Each of the adrenals has two parts: an outer cortex and an inner medulla.

In response to the release of adrenocorticotropic hormone (ACTH, which stimulates the release of cortisol) from the pituitary gland, the cortex secretes a number of steroid hormones that directly affect the balance of salt, water and glucose in the body. Cortisol is usually secreted by the adrenal cortex and affects glucose metabolism according to our daily sleep and wake

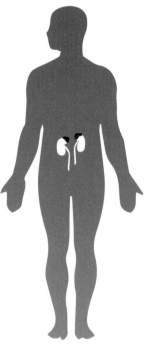

Adrenal glands

76

cycle; its concentration in the blood is much higher during the day than it is at night. During a stress response, cortisol secretion rises in proportion to the degree of stress; this is more marked when the stress arises from physical injury. Cortisol increases the concentration of glucose in our body by breaking down proteins, fats and carbohydrates. As a result, stress increases the level of blood sugar, an appropriate response to acute stress to ensure adequate energy supply for both the brain and skeletal muscles at a time when immediate physical activity may be required.

Besides ACTH, the pituitary produces endorphins and other related compounds. The precise mode of operation of these compounds is still not completely clear; however, it is assumed their pain-relieving properties, along with other postulated effects on mood and perception, may combine to allow life-saving exertions by a person despite serious injury, which is similar to acts of heroism in extreme danger situations.

The adrenal medulla is intimately associated with the sympathetic nervous system. Its main secretion — adrenaline — is related to noradrenaline, one of the most important neurotransmitters of the sympathetic system. Adrenaline secretion is initiated by direct stimulation of the adrenal medulla by the sympathetic nerves.

Exposure to a stressor produces an immediate increase in sympathetic nerve activity, which in turn results in the release of significant quantities of adrenaline from the adrenal medulla into the bloodstream, thereby preparing the body for fight or flight. Once this hormone is released into the blood it can quickly permeate the tissues of the body, augmenting the activity of sympathetic nerves. The effects of this are well known: increased heart rate and breathing rate, palpitation, trembling, hair rising and so on. Along with these predominantly physical responses, the feedback to the brain arouses an emotional response to stress that is normally manifested as some degree of fearfulness and anxiety, therefore impacting the base root, solar plexus and heart chakras.

Gonads

The gonads, including testes and ovaries, are associated with the muladhara (base root) and swadhisthana (sacral) chakras. The physical aspect of sex and sexuality is connected with muladhara, while the physiological aspect is connected to swadhisthana. Adrenal fatigue or depletion of physical energy affects physical relationships.

The gonads play an important role as hormone-producing endocrine organs, responsible for producing sperm and egg cells. The manufacture and release of sex hormones in both the sexes during reproductive life is controlled by the hypothalamus and pituitary glands, in much the same way they control other endocrine organs. Acute and chronic emotional stress can affect the balance of the female reproductive system, leading to hormonal imbalances and irregularities of the menstrual cycle along with a disturbance or inhibition of ovulation. This is quite common in the presence of both physical and emotional stressors. Men are also affected by emotional and physical stress, which can lead to common sexual dysfunction such as difficulties with erection and premature ejaculation and sometimes affect sperm production, causing infertility.

Pancreas

Most of the pancreas is non-endocrine in nature, being concerned with producing digestive juices for the gut. Its function is regulated by the manipura (solar plexus) chakra. The pancreas is situated behind the stomach. Embedded within the bulk of its tissue lie numerous clusters of endocrine cells called islets of Langerhans that secrete insulin and glucagon, two substances with essentially complementary actions in the maintenance of normal glucose levels. Insulin lowers blood sugar levels by encouraging body cells to absorb more glucose, and raises blood sugar levels by mobilising the sizeable store of carbohydrates present in the liver and converting it to glucose.

Thymus gland

The thymus gland, which is regulated by the anahata (heart) chakra, is called a gland although it is now accepted that its primary function is regulatory, mainly for the immune system. It is most active before birth and during early life, after which it reduces in size. Despite its size in adult life it continues to secrete significant volumes of the hormone thymosin, which regulates the immune level.

The thymus is responsible for the initiation and maintenance of the immune response, underlying the importance of the heart chakra's role in health maintenance. Thymosin is responsible for the production and programming of T-cells (a type of white blood cell), which can distinguish between the body's own protein and that

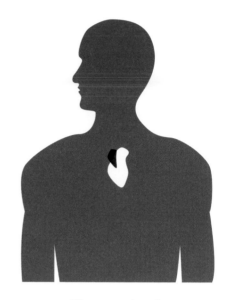

Thymus gland

of foreign origin such as invading germs and bacteria or genetically mutated cells. When the system identifies such foreign proteins it can mobilise resources to destroy and remove them. Thymosin is also involved in the maintenance of T-cell function; malfunction or maldevelopment of T-cells leads to overwhelming infection or the uncontrolled multiplication of mutated cells, which may manifest as cancer or auto-immune disease or HIV/AIDS.

Thyroid gland

The thyroid gland is shaped like a butterfly or a bowtie and is located across the front of the upper part of the trachea (windpipe). It is associated with the vishuddhi (throat) chakra. The thyroid is responsible for the manufacture of hormones, which are released into the bloodstream to control the rate of metabolism (the process of oxygen uptake and subsequent production of energy and heat within the body) in all the other tissues and organs. While all other endocrine glands produce their secretions when required, the thyroid stores within itself almost three months' supply of its hormones. In most people thyroid production is controlled within fairly narrow limits, but severe stress exposure may result in increased production. The vishuddhi chakra, which is related to communication and self-expression, is easily affected by emotional stress and bottled emotions, which may have a direct or indirect effect on the thyroid gland as well as the sacral and heart chakras.

Pineal gland

This small organ (6 mm x 4 mm) lies deep within the brain and appears at around the 36th day of gestation. It gains maximum development at around seven years of age and undergoes involution by the age of 14. Pinealocytes, the main cells contained in the pineal gland, are responsible for the production of melatonin, which regulates sleep and wakefulness in synchrony with the dark/light cycle. The balance of this delicate rhythm is easily upset by events such as changing time zones, going on night duty and stress, causing sleep disturbance. Pinealocytes are necessary for the development and functioning of gonads, pituitary and thyroids.

Although considered to be a part of the brain, the pineal gland is outside the brain blood barrier and lacks true nerve cells. It is associated with the sahasrara (crown) chakra.

5

Lymphatic system

As mentioned earlier, vital energy or pranas circulate in the body through the nervous system, the circulatory system and the nadis. The circulatory system has two aspects: the blood circulatory system and the lymphatic system. Blood moves through the body in closed vessels, arteries and veins, while lymph moves via lymphatic vessels, which are like open channels in the body. While the movement of blood is regulated by the pumping of the heart, lymph movement is mainly due to muscle activity. A sedentary lifestyle adversely affects our lymphatic flow and makes it sluggish. However, other factors that affect our lymphatic system adversely are emotional blockages and stress. We have observed this over a period of time while working with clients with lymph-related issues. We could establish an interesting correlation between emotional blockages, lymphatic blockages and chakra health.

The lymphatic system has not been given enough attention by the medical world, nor has there been any significant study or research to analyse lymphatic movement and the causes of lymph blockages. Medical doctors are sometimes clueless in understanding the causes of and treatment for lymphatic blockages and swollen lymph nodes, which can often be cleared simply by manual lymph drainage, a technique used by massage therapists.

As explained in the section on vayus (the role of the energy in each chakra), there are five variants of energy associated with the different chakras. The energy associated with the swadhisthana (sacral) chakra is vyana vayu, which controls fluid circulation in the body. The swadhisthana chakra is associated with the water element, an element that represents all the fluids in the body, including lymph. Therefore, it can be concluded that the swadhisthana chakra influences lymphatic flow in the body.

To understand this concept, we need to understand the lymphatic system and lymph nodes. In short, lymph is all the interstitial fluid, or the fluid between the cells. This fluid basically oozes out from the arteries at the extremities. Our arterial blood carries oxygen, nutrients and hormones for all the cells in the body. To reach the cells at the extremities lymph leaves the small arteries and flows into the tissues,

Cervical lymph nodes

Tonsil

Supraclavicular lymph nodes

Thymus

Thoracic duct

Mediastinal lymph Nodes

Axillary lymph nodes

Spleen

Cubital nodes

Cisterna chyli

Lymphatic vessels

Retroperitoneal lymph nodes

Inguinal lymph nodes

Pelvic lymph nodes

Bone marrow

Popliteal lymph nodes

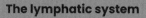

The lymphatic system

filling the space between the cells. This fluid delivers its nourishing products to the cells then leaves the cells, taking with it toxins and waste products. It is composed of 97 per cent water and almost 3 per cent of white blood corpuscles and lymphocytes. Lymph contains less proteins and oxygen than blood plasma and doesn't have any red corpuscles (erythrocytes). Our lymphatic system is a secondary circulatory system that supplies nutrients and drains the tissue fluids and toxins from the tissue spaces.

The lymphatic system is mainly responsible for the following functions:

- removing excess fluid and waste products from the interstitial spaces between the cells
- aiding the immune system by removing and destroying waste, debris, dead blood cells, pathogens, toxins and cancer cells
- absorbing fats and fat-soluble vitamins from the digestive system and delivering these nutrients to the cells of the body.

Lymph moves in the interstitial spaces up to the subclavian veins at the base of the neck. Approximately 70 per cent of these veins are superficial capillaries located near or just under the skin. The remaining 30 per cent, which are known as deep lymphatic capillaries, surround most of the body's organs.

Lymph nodes generally occur in groups at various parts of the body, such as under the knee, groin or inguinal area under the arm or neck. The task of the lymph nodes is to control the lymph transported to it. Every lymph node, which is only a few millimetres in diameter, consists of lymphatic tissue enclosed in a covering of connective tissue. All lymph nodes have the primary function of the production of lymphocytes, which help defend the body against microorganisms and harmful foreign particles and remove debris from lymph before it is returned to the bloodstream.

The major lymph nodes are mainly found in six areas:

- **Cervical region:** nodes in this area are grouped along the lower border of the jaw, in front of and behind the ears, and deep in the neck along the larger blood vessels. They drain the skin of the scalp and face, the tissues of the nasal cavity and the pharynx. This area is associated with the vishuddhi (throat) chakra.

- **Axillary region:** these nodes are in the underarm region and receive lymph from vessels that drain the arm, the walls of the thorax, the breast and the upper walls of the abdomen. This area is associated with the anahata (heart) chakra.

- **Inguinal region:** the nodes in this area receive lymph from the legs, the outer portion of the genitalia and the lower abdominal wall. This area is under the influence of the swadhisthana (sacral) chakra. The health of these lymph nodes and the health of the sacral chakra are interrelated as both affect each other. The sacral chakra is the one that indirectly controls lymphatic circulation as the energy associated with it, called vyana vayu, regulates fluid circulation in the body.

- **Pelvic cavity:** the nodes here appear mostly along the paths of the blood vessels within the pelvic cavity and receive lymph from the lymphatic vessels in the area. This area is also associated with the swadhisthana and muladhara (base root) chakras.

- **Abdominal cavity:** within this area, nodes occur in chains along the main branches of the arteries of the intestine and the abdominal aorta. This area is associated with the manipura (solar plexus) chakra.

- **Thoracic cavity:** these nodes occur between the lungs and along the windpipe and bronchi, and receive lymph from this area and from the internal wall of the thorax. This area is also associated with the anahata (heart) chakra.

The idea that 'our issues are in our tissues' is indeed true, as all emotional issues get stuck and are stored somewhere in the body. Our minds tend to forget bitter experiences over time but they remain imbedded somewhere in the body's memory. Over the years of our chakra healing practice we have noticed these issues show up as knots in the muscles in the inguinal area, just above or below the inguinal lymph nodes; they lead to blockages of the inguinal nodes. In the same way these emotional blockages may also show up as knots on the sides of the breast and under the bra line, affecting the heart chakra and axillary nodes.

Emotional and mental stress and blockages mainly affect the energies and vibrations of the sacral, heart and throat chakras. Prolonged stress affecting the energies of these chakras may cause sluggishness and congestion of lymphatic flow in the inguinal, axillary and sub-mandibular region. Congestion in inguinal nodes may result in fluid retention and lower back pain, and may also affect the reproductive organs and lead to menstrual imbalances, uterine fibroids, endometriosis and fertility issues.

If a person has an inability to express emotions it can affect thyroid function and lymph circulation in the sub-mandibular area or the jaw line, manifesting as congestion on the chin and face. This also affects the lymph nodes in the front and back of the ears, resulting in problems such as tinnitus (ringing of the ears).

The sacral chakra has a direct bearing on the heart chakra, since emotional issues also involve the heart and can affect lymph circulation in that area. Blockages of the axillary lymph nodes in the underarms may cause swelling or lumps in the area and lymphatic congestion in the chest area, leading to mastalgia, fibrocystic breast conditions or even breast cancer. This aspect of health and the process of disease needs more research and investigation, which may give us insight into the unexplained causes of various health problems including cancer.

6

Chakra aspects and symbols

Tantra and eastern yogic systems describe the presence of seven major chakras between the head and up to the base of the torso that correspond to the major nerve plexuses in the body, while also acknowledging the presence of varying numbers of minor chakras all over the body. This part of the body houses our major organs and glands, and the energy metabolism of these organs and glands is responsible for chakra formation.

Each of the major chakras has two aspects: one on the front of the body, the ventral aspect, and its counterpart on the back of the body, the dorsal aspect. These can be considered as the front and rear aspects of the chakras, and are known as vortices (openings). The muladhara (base root) chakra and the sahasrara (crown) chakra — the first at the bottom and the last at the crown — have just one funnel-like opening; they are termed single-vortex chakras. The other five chakras have front and back openings and are known as double-vortice chakras.

The front or ventral aspect of the chakras is related to feelings, while the back or dorsal aspect is related to the will. Since the ventral aspect is associated with feelings it is considered to be highly sensitive, therefore it is recommended that healing work is performed from the dorsal side of a client. Self-healing can, however, be done from the front. It is also interesting to note that at the lower part of the body the muladhara and swadhisthana chakras are connected at a T-junction, as are the ajna and sahasrara chakras.

In tantra symbology, each of the chakras is associated with a symbol that depicts different aspects and has a spiritual relevance:

- the number of petals of the lotus flower
- colour
- animal
- deity
- yantra, or geometric shape
- bija mantra.

See Chapter 8 for the specific symbol of each chakra.

In tantra practice each chakra has a specific number of petals denoting the vibration frequency; the higher the number of petals the finer the vibration. In Hindu spiritual practices the lotus flower is highly revered and is used with most of the deities. The lotus plant is considered to be the best example of spiritual ascension since the plant grows in mud, symbolising tamas or ignorance; moves up through water, symbolising rajas or endeavour and aspiration; and eventually reaches out of the water and blooms under the light of the sun, symbolising sattva or illumination. Thus the lotus symbolises the evolution of man from the lowest state of awareness (tamas) to the highest state of consciousness (sattva).

Ancient sages envisioned the chakras as moving energy centres and assigned particular colours to each one. In their 1988 research, Dr Valerie Hunt and associates stated that the chakras frequently follow the same colour patterns as mentioned in tantric and metaphysical literature (see Chapter 2).

In the chakra system animals are an objective representation symbolising the psychological meaning of the individual chakra. For instance, in muladhara the elephant represents stability and memory of previous births. In astrology animals are assigned to various zodiac signs, and Chinese astrology is also based on animal symbols. Certain chakra healers also recommend visualisation of the animals and colours associated with each chakra to draw in the healing vibrations for that chakra.

Hindu deities are also assigned to various chakras; they represent the energy vibrations resonating with a particular chakra. For example, the elephant god Ganesha is the ruling deity of muladhara, as he represents Earth energy. Ancient sages recommended praying to him at the beginning of any religious or spiritual ritual, which is still practised, to help remove obstacles in the ritual as well as in life. Even the deity's energy can be drawn upon by praying to the yantra (sacred geometry drawn according to the vibrations of the deity). However, the best yantra to pray with is shri yantra, which has nine interlaced triangles of yin and yang with a point in the centre; this is the point of connection with higher consciousness. Meditating on shri yantra is recommended, keeping the focus on this point to establish a connection with higher consciousness.

A bija or seed mantra is a single-syllable sound. 'Bija' means 'seed', and like tiny seeds they have all the wisdom of a tree. A bija mantra contains spiritual wisdom; it is the creative force and has the vibrations of a whole verse (mantra). Each chakra is assigned to a particular bija mantra such as 'lam', 'vam', 'ram', 'yam', 'hum' or 'aum/om'. The primordial sound of the universe, aum has three letters. Chanting 'a-u-m' generates two vibrations; the first aspect in the beginning produces the sound of 'aa', which can be prolonged as 'aa … uuuu … nnnnnnnnnnnnnnnnn . . .' and ending 'm', which marks the culmination. After that the mouth closes. Chanting 'aum' regularly leads us to a meditative state.

During a chakra meditation it is recommended we chant a bija mantra while keeping focus on the associated chakra, then move our breath vibrations and energy to the respective chakra point. For detailed guidance on chakra meditation see Chapter 9.

Each of the chakras is depicted as a set of lotus petals; for example, the muladhara (base root) chakra is depicted as a four-petalled lotus, the swadhisthana (sacral) chakra is depicted as a six-petalled lotus and so on. A Sanskrit letter is depicted on each of the petals and is associated with the particular chakra. The Sanskrit language has 50 letters, each of which is inscribed on each petal of the chakra from the root to the third eye chakra. The last four letters of the alphabet are inscribed on the four petals of the root chakra.

7

Chakra numbers and planets

When a child is conceived in its mother's womb and starts growing from a unicellular being to a multicellular one, the first organ to develop is the brain and particularly the hypothalamus. At this stage the sahasrara (crown) chakra opens. The crown chakra is our connection to higher consciousness, and with its opening our individual consciousness flows in. This consciousness comes with the complete blueprint of the child to come in this material world. According to Hindu philosophy this blueprint is based on our past-life karma and carries information about our destiny in this lifetime. An astrologer deciphers this blueprint by understanding planetary positions at the time of birth. Palmists read the lines on the palm, numerologists calculate birth/life numbers and psychics use their intuition. All these tools and methods are used to read the map of consciousness, which also proves that the universe and our psyche are not random or chaotic but that there is a certain order and structure to them.

There are hidden numerical patterns that serve as keys for unlocking the secrets of the psyche. According to numerology, each number is associated with a particular planet and planetary influences affect our life and also the chakras. While exploring the fundamentals of form and frequency, the Greek philosopher and mathematician Pythagoras discovered relationships between mind and matter. He pointed to the hidden numerical patterns that served as keys for unlocking the secrets of the psyche, mystically associating numbers with virtues, colours and many other ideas. Astrologers added to this knowledge by associating planets to numbers. While assessing chakras over a period of time we had been looking for certain common denominators to understand the forces that shape the human psyche and personality, and we also found the key in numerology. By studying clients' birth and life path numbers and the association with a certain planet and their influence on each chakra we establish certain patterns and temperaments affecting particular chakras.

We observed that numbers and planets have an influence on a person's life and personality that is also reflected in their temperament and attitude towards life and in turn their chakra energies. For example, the number 1 is ruled by the sun, which influences the manipura (solar plexus) chakra. Temperamentally, people with the number 1 as their birth or life path number are over-ambitious in life, over-using their manipura chakra. These people have signs and symptoms of an overactive manipura chakra and are prone to conditions such as acid reflux, headaches/migraines, high cholesterol, hypertension or high blood sugar. In the chart below we have demonstrated which numbers and planets have association with each of the chakras. If a practitioner can figure out the birth and life path numbers, they should look into the related chakras for imbalances and help the clients accordingly:

- **muladhara** (base root) chakra: planet Mars; number 9

- **swadhisthana** (sacral) chakra: planets Venus, moon, Rahu, Ketu; numbers 2, 4, 6, 7

- **manipura** (solar plexus) chakra: planets Jupiter, sun; numbers 1, 3

- **anahata** (heart) chakra: planets Mercury, Venus; numbers 5, 6

- **vishuddhi** (throat) chakra: planets Mercury, Rahu, Ketu; numbers 4, 5, 7

- **ajna** (third eye) chakra: planets Jupiter, Saturn; numbers 3, 8

- **sahasrara** (crown) chakra: planet Saturn; number 8.

8

Chakra attributes

In this chapter we have tried to put each aspect and attribute of the individual chakras in perspective so you can understand the whole picture. We have explained the causes and results of imbalances along with the choice of healing tools, mainly in terms of essential oils and crystals.

Muladhara (base root)

Guna: tamas	
Element: earth	
Vayu: apana	
Auric layer: physical/etheric body	
Colour: crimson red	
Structural representation: four petals	
Bija mantra: lam	
Developmental age: one to seven years	
Main issues: survival, physical needs	
Glands: adrenal and gonads	
Site: perineum (corresponds to the coccyx)	
Sense: smell	
Sense organ: nose	
Work organ: anus	
Animal: elephant	

Deity: Ganesha

Number: 9

Planet: Mars

Zodiac sign: Capricorn

Essential oils: jatamansi (Indian spikenard), patchouli, valerian root, nagarmotha (nutgrass), vetiver, costus root oils

Crystals: coral, jasper, haematite, black/brown/moss agate, red garnet

107

Traditionally, the subtle body or aura is considered to be formed of seven layers, each corresponding and sequentially related to a definite chakra. The first layer of the energy field over our physical body, the etheric body (the etheric state between energy and matter), is connected to our first chakra or the muladhara (base root) chakra. This layer is associated with automatic and autonomic functions of the body, as muladhara is associated with physical functioning and physical sensations of feeling, whether it's pain or pleasure.

Muladhara is the first chakra in the spiritual evolution of man, where a person goes beyond animal consciousness and starts to be a real human. Located at the perineum (between the anus and the genitals) at the area of the pelvic plexus, this chakra represents the grounding of a being in the material world. It represents the will to survive and acts as an energy pump. Within it lies dormant kundalini energy, representing the physical potency and vitality of the person in whom it is active.

The muladhara chakra represents a person's basic nature (mool prakriti). It is the manifestation of the individual consciousness into human form. This chakra is dominant during the first seven years of a child's life and is responsible for physical development. During these first seven years a child is self-centred and highly concerned with their physical survival and security. This is the phase in which an infant grounds itself and adapts to the laws of the world, learning to regulate patterns of eating, drinking and sleeping and securing a worldly identity. An imbalance of this chakra during this early phase of life may result in physical problems, deformity or even insecurity.

The muladhara chakra is depicted as a four-petalled lotus of a crimson red colour. Tantric scriptures state that each of the petals has letters written in gold: 'vam', 'sha', 'sham' and 'sam' – the last four letters of the Sanskrit alphabet. There is a yellow square in the pericarp of the lotus flower, which symbolises the earth element. The yellow square is supported by an elephant with seven trunks. The elephant represents strength and solidity, and the seven trunks denote the seven minerals vital to physical functioning as well as memories of the past seven lives as the muladhara chakra also carries the imprints of our past lives.

In the centre of the lotus fire is symbolised by an inverted red triangle; on top of the triangle is the bija mantra for muladhara, which is *lam*. Hindu philosophy associates Ganesha as the ruling deity for this chakra. Another name for Ganesha is 'Ganapati', Gana being the guardian deity of eight directions and *pati* meaning 'nurturer'; thus Ganapati/Ganesha is the lord of all directions.

Ganesha belongs to Shiva's family. According to Hindu mythology, he was created by Shiva's consort Parvati out of mud and her body dirt. She invoked life in the boy, called him her son and directed him to guard the entrance of her home. She instructed him not to allow anyone inside the house while she was gone for her bath. During this period Shiva returned home but was not allowed to enter as he was not known to Ganesha. Shiva tried to reason with Ganesha but Ganesha was adamant; a confrontation followed and Shiva, out of anger, beheaded the young boy and entered the house.

Later, Parvati made him realise his mistake of beheading their own son and insisted that Shiva revive the boy. When Shiva agreed to her demand, the head of the boy disappeared mysteriously. Shiva sent his soldiers to find the boy's head, or any head. The soldiers went to the jungle, found a baby elephant sleeping with his head towards north and beheaded the elephant after seeking his permission. This head was then placed on the boy's shoulders and life was invoked in the boy again. The boy was named Ganesha and blessed by all the gods as Pratham Pujya (first worshipped). Since that time in all Hindu rituals and prayers, Ganesha is invoked and prayed to first.

The relevance of the baby elephant being beheaded while sleeping with its head in the north can be found in fundamental principles of vastu, the ancient Indian science of structures and dwelling units. According to vastu shastra, our heads represent the North Pole and our feet the South Pole. When we sleep with our head in the north it causes a disturbance in the body's biomagnetic fluids and affects our health, which is why ancient Indian scriptures describe north as the direction of death and recommend not sleeping with the head towards north.

However, from a spiritual point of view north is the direction of the gods, especially the lord of wealth, Kuber.

The muladhara chakra is the core of our physical existence. As our physical body is the carrier of our soul, we can say our physical body is our soulmate. As long as we are embodied, our primary responsibility is to take care of the physical body.

The muladhara chakra represents our grounding in the physical world. According to Ayurveda and tantra, it is associated with the earth element. As mentioned previously, we are the microcosm of the macrocosm. Mother Earth represents the macrocosm, which is made up of minerals, metals, flora and fauna. Our physical body is the microcosm, representing the balance of minerals, metals, flora and fauna. Any imbalance of these may lead to health problems; for example, a deficiency of calcium can cause bone problems and arthritis, an iron deficiency can lead to immune system problems and magnesium, potassium, zinc and selenium all affect our muscles and physical body. The source of nourishment of the physical body is the food we eat; whether the food is vegetarian or non-vegetarian, it all comes from the Earth.

Earth is an important element for the grounding of trees and for human beings to stay healthy and grounded in life. Grounding actually means to be focused in whatever activity we are engaged in. When our mind is preoccupied or drifts to something else and away from the task in hand, we are prone to making mistakes and will face obstacles in life. Those who are unstable in life and not able to hold on to jobs and relationships and who change residences often need grounding. They need to work to strengthen their muladhara chakra.

Ancient Indian sages were able to visualise chakras and chakra imbalances, and they suggested simple remedies to correct the imbalances. To strengthen the muladhara chakra they would prescribe a daily bare foot visit to a pipal or banyan tree (both are renowned for their strong and healthy roots). They also suggested offering water and walking seven times around the tree. Some people considered this all to be superstition, but walking bare footed on the ground around plants with strong roots helps with grounding and strengthening of the root chakra.

The muladhara chakra is also associated with our sense of smell, the most primordial and basic of the senses. This chakra is the highest chakra in animals, which have a very well-developed sense of smell.

The vayu or energy associated with this chakra is apana vayu, the energy of elimination. Physiologically, this chakra is related to elimination processes, controls the urinary, sexual and reproductive organs, influences large intestine functions and bowel movement and regulates the adrenals and gonads. Apana vayu works as a flush valve so that we can control elimination at will; when we can't control elimination there is a leakage of this energy that leads to incontinence or chronic or adrenal fatigue, making us feel weak and drained.

Imbalances and the tools to heal them

Since this chakra governs our physical body it is responsible for everything about our physical body: skin, hair, the immune and skeletal systems and accompanying physical complaints or disease. It is responsible for skin problems such as allergies, eczema and psoriasis, regenerative powers, irregular bowel movement and renal system problems, resulting in things such as brittle bones, frequent illness, delayed recovery from common ailments, accident proneness, arthritis, constipation, fistula, fissures and haemorrhoids. Some other related diseases are cancer, leukaemia, sexual ailments, retarded physical growth and psychological problems.

According to Patanjali, yoga is a system that aligns mind, body and spirit. Hatha yoga exercises are designed to help our physical bodies to stay healthy and flexible and strengthen our chakras. All light physical exercises have a soma-psychic effect as they improve breathing and provide us with the ability to manage mental and emotional stress. Kriya yoga recommends mula bandha, a pelvic floor exercise similar to Kegel that specifically strengthens this chakra and helps to control incontinence.

The recommended crystals are any that are coloured red, such as red jasper and red garnet, along with haematite and all black-coloured stones such as black tourmaline, black obsidian and black onyx. These all help to strengthen this chakra and provide grounding.

Aromatherapy essential oils are effective for chakra healing and activation. To pick the right essential oils for the muladhara chakra, look for oils that represent earth energy. Since the oils from the roots of the plant resonate with earth vibrations, they are best suited for this chakra's healing and balancing. Jatamansi, or Indian spikenard, was used by Mary Magdalene to massage Jesus Christ's feet before the last supper. Other useful oils to strengthen this chakra are patchouli, vetiver, valerian toot and angelica root.

Swadhisthana (sacral)

Guna: rajas	
Element: water	
Vayu: vyana	
Auric layer: emotional body	
Colour: vermilion orange	
Structural representation: six petals	
Bija mantra: vam	
Developmental age: seven to 14 years	
Main issues: emotional balance, sexuality	
Gland: gonads	
Site: cervix or the sacral plexus in the pubic region	
Sense: taste	
Sense organ: tongue	
Work organ: genitals	
Animal: crocodile	

Deities: Shakti, Durga

Numbers: 2, 4, 6, 7

Planets: moon, Venus, Rahu, Ketu

Zodiac signs: Cancer, Scorpio

Essential oils: sandalwood, clary sage, cedarwood, ginger, juniper berry, cypress, jasmine

Crystals: carnelian, pearl, mother of pearl, hessonite garnet, orange or honey calcite, moonstone

The swadhisthana (sacral) chakra is dominant between the ages of seven to 14, the phase of life associated with puberty and preparation of the body, physically and physiologically, for procreation. This is the period that sensuality enters in a child's relationships, allowing them to reach out to family and friends as a new awareness of the physical body evolves. During this phase a child also undergoes emotional development, hence it is associated with our emotional body. This chakra denotes the desire centre of a being.

The Sanskrit word 'swadhisthana' comprises *swa*, meaning 'one's own', and *adhisthan*, meaning 'dwelling place'; it represents the true nature of a person. Also, the term *swad* means 'taste', which is the sense associated with this chakra. This chakra is considered to be the desire centre of our being — desires not just of physical or sexual natures but all material desires are tasted. Desires are not needs, but they do rule some of us. When we fulfil one desire another one crops up, leaving us always unsatisfied and wanting. When the desires are uncontrollable we call them addictions; all addictions result from an imbalance in this chakra. Our desires are distractions in the path of our spiritual progress; they play at a person's mind, making them restless and confused. As long as we are ruled by our desires we will never be happy and satisfied in life.

This chakra is related to procreation, material desires, emotionality and emotional balance. Positioned at the pubic region, it regulates the gonads and sex organs and is responsible for the quality and quantity of sexual energy, as well as its exchange between self and others at physical, emotional and spiritual planes.

It is depicted as a six-petalled lotus of vermilion orange colour. The Sanskrit letters 'bam', 'bham', 'mam', 'yam' , 'ram' and 'lam' are written on each of the petals. Within the pericarp of the lotus is a white crescent moon. The animal associated with swadhisthana is the crocodile, which represents the unconscious mind and its sensuous nature. Seated on the crocodile is the bija mantra *vam*. Within the bindu of the mantra is depicted the deities Vishnu and Rakini as a form of shakti. Vishnu is the sustainer of the universe and represents the power of preservation. Rakini shakti is depicted with two heads, representing the duality of energy in this chakra whereby a person is trying to attain a balance between the world outside and the world within.

Ayurveda and tantra associate the water element with this chakra. Our Earth is two-thirds water, and our bodies are made up of two-thirds water. The water on Earth is affected by lunar cycles, with the moon phases being responsible for high and low tides, and our bodies are also affected by moon phases. This is why some people experience mood swings, particularly during a full moon, and why this chakra is considered to be the seat of emotional balance.

According to tantra our unconscious minds record each and every perception, association and experience, with a quarrel or bitterness having a stronger registration. These registrations play a part in determining our day-to-day behaviour, attitudes and reactions and create a hindrance to our spiritual progress.

The vayu associated with this chakra is vyana vayu, which regulates circulation of the fluids in the body whether it's blood, lymph, saliva or menstrual fluids. Physiologically, swadhisthana regulates our reproductive, urinary and lymphatic systems, corresponds to the hypogastric or sacral plexus of nerves and controls the unconscious in human beings.

Imbalances and the tools to heal them

Emotional stress is the major cause of imbalances or blockages in this chakra. It may also be the cause of chronic depression, resulting in malfunctioning of the circulatory system and especially the lymphatic system. It also affects the excretory system of the body, resulting in problems with body fluids such as blood, lymph, saliva, urine and menstrual flow and all the organs related to their production. At the physiological level, an imbalance of the sacral chakra can affect hormone production, leading to menstrual problems and issues with fertility.

Swadhisthana is the seat of emotional balance and also influences the heart and throat chakras. An inability to express emotions can affect thyroid function and lymph circulation in the sub-mandibular area or the jaw line, manifesting as congestion on the chin and face; it also affects the lymph nodes in the front and back of the ears and may cause tinnitus. This chakra has a direct bearing on the heart chakra, since emotional issues also involve the heart. A heart chakra imbalance affects lymph circulation in that area, causing breast problems or even breast cancer. A weak or imbalanced sacral chakra is also the cause of compulsive-obsessive behaviour and addictions.

The practice of mula bandha yoga (anal/genital contractions similar to Kegel exercises) is effective in strengthening this chakra. A gentle massage on a regular basis with the flat of the fingers in the inguinal lymph nodes area will help clear chakra congestion and move circulation and energies.

Among the healing crystals, carnelian is popular for the sacral chakra as its balancing energies help to move fluids in the body. Other useful stones are orange agate and orange calcite. Hessonite garnet is also a powerful gem stone to heal and balance the sacral chakra.

Among the essential oils we prefer using those that represent the water element. In plants the water element is represented in the stems or the wood, as they are the water channels; therefore, we use oils from the stems and wood. Sandalwood is a powerful essential oil, while other useful oils are cedarwood, ginger, rosewood and juniper berry. Pure jasmine absolute has been clinically tried as an emotional balancer and anti-depressant, besides being an aphrodisiac.

Manipura (solar plexus)

Guna: rajas	
Element: fire	
Vayu: samana	
Auric layer: mental body	
Colour: yellow	
Structural representation: 10 petals	
Bija mantra: ram	
Developmental age: 14 to 21 years	
Main issues: mental power, self-will, ambitions	
Gland: pancreas	
Site: below the diaphragm, representing the solar plexus	
Sense: sight	
Sense organ: eyes	
Work organs: feet and legs	
Animal: ram	

Deity: Ram (reincarnation of Lord Vishnu)

Numbers: 1, 3, 7

Planets: sun, Jupiter, Ketu

Zodiac signs: Aries, Leo

Essential oils: black pepper, rosemary, chamomile, juniper berry, marjoram, turmeric, thyme

Crystals: ruby, tiger's eye, yellow topaz, citrine, yellow calcite, pyrite, sunstone

The manipura (solar plexus) chakra is associated with the mental body in our auric layer. It corresponds to the solar plexus, which is the seat of our personal power. This chakra controls the entire process of digestion, assimilation and temperature regulation at the physical level. It is most dominant during the age of 14 to 21 years, a phase of life during which a person tries to seek their identity in the world. This chakra also represents our lower mind, as it is responsible for our life ambitions, drive, mental power, logical thinking, reasoning and power-seeking attitude. This chakra governs the establishment of the ego in the human realms, with varying degrees of self-assertion and its acceptability. The organs of action are the feet and legs, underlying the interdependence of vision with the wilful actions of the legs and feet.

The Sanskrit word 'manipura' derives from *mani*, meaning 'jewel', and *pura*, meaning 'city'; literally, it means 'city of jewels'. In Tibetan tradition it is referred to as the jewelled lotus mani padma. It is the seat of life ambitions, money, power, self-will, self-assertion and authority and ego. A person with a dominant solar plexus chakra will strive for personal power and recognition, even to the detriment of family and friends. These are the traits of people with the number 1 as their birth or life number.

Manipura is symbolised as a 10-petalled lotus, with the Sanskrit letters 'pham', 'dam', 'dham', 'nam', 'tam', 'tham', 'dam', 'dham', 'nam' and 'pam' on each petal. In the centre of the lotus is the region of fire, which is symbolised by an inverted fiery red triangle that shines like a rising sun. In the lower apex of the triangle is the ram, vehicle of the bija, which symbolises dynamism and indomitable endurance. On this is placed the seed mantra 'ram'. In the Indian scripture *Ramayan*, Shri Ram, around whom the whole epic revolves, comes from the lineage of the sun and is hence called Suryavanshi. The element associated with this chakra is fire, represented by the sun. The sun was a raja (king), and this chakra is rajasic; the seed mantra is his name, Ram, which is a very powerful mantra for the solar plexus chakra.

The sense associated with this chakra is sight, as our optic nerve is influenced by it. Manipura is associated with the fire element, which aids in complete metabolic processes including digestion and the absorption of food in order to provide our bodies the vital energy they need for their survival. The vayu associated with this chakra is samana vayu. According to sawar yoga (the yoga of breath), this chakra is an important junction where prana and apana vayu meet, maintaining the balance of vital forces.

Manipura is responsible for the expression of individuality, and it is here that the dissolution of karmic account begins on the path of spirituality. This chakra is considered to be the last peak of the mortal plane or the physical plane of existence. Kundalini tantra states that kundalini rises in all of us from the muladhara (base root) chakra up to the manipura (solar plexus) chakra, as the lower three chakras are responsible for fulfilling our basic needs. Once the kundalini crosses manipura and reaches the anahata (heart) chakra, the process of spiritual awakening begins. It is believed that once kundalini crosses the astral bridge, which is the energetic barrier between manipura and anahata, it only moves upwards, taking the sadhaka (spiritual practitioner) to a higher spiritual realm.

According to tantric and Buddhist traditions the actual awakening process of kundalini happens at manipura, not at muladhara. As long as the evolution is at the level of the muladhara and swadhisthana chakras the aspirant is stuck in the mundane, like a lotus is in the mud. Here the mud represents our own physical needs, desires and mental and emotional problems. As soon as the seeker transcends to manipura and detaches from material desires they can see the whole perspective of things and all the possibilities of human consciousness.

This is the same concept described by the famous psychologist Abraham Maslow in his hierarchy of human needs. According to Maslow, at the first level we all have basic or physiological needs for survival, which are common for both human beings and animals. These needs include food, sex and shelter and are ruled by the lower three chakras. The next level is safety needs, again ruled by muladhara, which is responsible for our fight or flight response. Above that level are our needs for belonging or the emotional needs, which are ruled by swadhisthana. After these needs are fulfilled we have the esteem or ego needs, which are ruled by manipura.

Once all of the basic needs are fulfilled but happiness is still elusive, then arises our spiritual need or the need for self-actualisation. This concept is similar to the concept of kundalini, the movement of which is initially through the lower chakras to fulfil the basic needs. Once kundalini crosses the astral bridge (the energetic barrier between the solar plexus and heart chakras) our spiritual journey begins.

Anatomically speaking, the solar plexus is a ganglion of nerves also known as the celiac plexus that is located in the V below the ribcage just below the diaphragm. The nerves travelling in the spinal column from the head meet at this V, with the nerves flowing freely in the lower part of the body. The nerves of the central nervous system have an insulating covering known as the myelin sheath; the nerves that come out from the spinal column do not have this insulation, which makes them prone to chemical changes in the body. A sudden reaction to mental or emotional stress will affect the body's biochemistry, leading to a sensation of butterflies in the tummy. Therefore, this chakra is known as the seat of anxieties.

Imbalances and the tools to heal them

An overactive solar plexus chakra is the cause of a heated liver, leading to a high body acid level. It also causes high cholesterol, hypertension, high blood pressure, acid reflux, headaches and migraines and even diabetes. This mostly happens when people are very ambitious in life, always chasing money, power or authority.

The need to gain undue and illogical supremacy creates imbalances and blockages in the functioning of this chakra, leading to raised levels of cholesterol and other conditions such as diabetes, ulcers, hepatitis, rheumatoid arthritis, heart diseases and bowel dysfunctions. If this chakra is unduly suppressed it causes imbalanced digestion, bad sleep and increased irritability. A weak solar plexus chakra is the cause of anxieties and excessive sweating on the palms and soles of the feet. If a person starts seeking atonement of their errors and moves towards a higher plane by following the path of dharma, then relief may be felt.

Yoga recommends abdominal breathing to soothe the solar plexus chakra. This area may feel knotted and tight when we push ourselves towards our life ambitions, and abdominal breathing will relieve that and promote better sleep. Alternate nostril breathing (anulom vilom) is recommended for everyone to keep this chakra and the sacral chakra in balance. It should be practised 11 to 21 times a day, morning or evening, deep and slow while maintaining focus on the breath. Kapalbhati (forehead brightener or breath of fire) is an exercise for the organs in the belly and activates the pancreas. It is also useful for diabetic people; however, some people feel it may increase blood pressure so you should be watchful.

All yellow crystals such as citrine, tiger's eye, pyrite, yellow calcite and yellow sapphire help to activate the solar plexus chakra.

However, if the solar plexus is already overactive then do not wear yellow, as it can aggravate the symptoms related to overactivity of the solar plexus such as acid reflux, headaches/migraines and hypertension. Those conditions need the cooling energy of green crystals.

When choosing essential oils for the solar plexus chakra we like those that represent the fire element, which is present in all spices and spice oils; they are good to activate the solar plexus. However, when the solar plexus is already overactive we use the cooling energy of green oils such as peppermint, spearmint and basil; these will soothe acid reflux and headaches and migraines.

Anahata (heart)

Guna: sattva
Element: air
Vayu: prana
Auric layer: astral body
Colours: green, pink
Structural representation: 12 petals
Bija mantra: yam
Developmental age: 21 to 28 years
Main issues: love, relationships
Gland: thymus
Site: at the centre and behind the sternum
Sense: touch
Sense organ: skin
Work organ: hands
Animal: antelope

Deities: Krishna, Vishnu

Numbers: 5, 6

Planets: Mercury, Venus

Zodiac signs: Libra, Taurus

Essential oils: holy basil, lavender, eucalyptus, tea tree, peppermint, spearmint, rosemary, rose, geranium

Crystals: malachite, peridot, rose quartz,emerald, watermelon tourmaline, green tourmaline, green aventurine, jade rhodochrosite, amazonite, kunzite, moldavite

The fourth energetic layer, the astral body, is associated with the very special anahata (heart) chakra. This layer is considered to be the bridge at the astral plane between the physical plane and the spiritual plane of existence. Most dominant during the ages of 21 to 28, this important chakra is the seat of our sustenance.

Anahata is about universal love, playing an important role in our relationships. Its proper functioning enables us to accept without conditions for ourselves and those around us, representing the goodness of humanity. At the physical and physiological levels this chakra corresponds to the cardiac plexus of nerves and controls the functions of the heart and diaphragm and other organs in the region, as well as regulating the function of the thymus gland.

In terms of chakra symbology, it is represented as a 12-petalled lotus. On each of the petals of the lotus are inscribed the letters 'kam', 'kham', 'gam', 'gham', 'ngam', 'cham', 'chhham', 'jam', 'jham', 'nyam', 'tam' and 'tham'. The inner region is hexagonal in shape and is made up of two interlaced triangles symbolising the union of Shiva and Shakti. The inverted triangle is the symbol of creativity (Shakti), while the upright triangle symbolises consciousness (Shiva). The hexagonal shape represents the air element.

The vehicle for the bija is the black antelope, which is known for its compassion, alertness and quick movement; it is placed in the centre of the hexagon, and above that is depicted the seed mantra 'yam'.

Within the centre are depicted the deities Ishana Rudra (Shiva), the lord of the north-east, and Kakini Shakti, the benefactress of all, auspicious and exhilarated. Below the main lotus of anahata is a subsidiary lotus with red petals that contains a wish-fulfilling tree called Kalpataru. When this tree starts to fructify your wishes begin to be realised.

Vishnu granthi is the second of the psychic knots located at the heart chakra. It represents the bondage of emotional attachments, which according to Patanjali's Yoga Sutras are major causes of imbalances in this chakra. Our attachments to people and things bring us only pain, anguish and trauma, as well as agony, but most of us consider our attachments to be love. When we have attachments we have expectations, and when the expectations are not fulfilled it causes pain or anguish. This chakra is about unconditional acceptance, and about love for humanity and all that forms the universe.

The Hindu scripture Bhagavad Gita is based on the sermon given by Lord Krishna to his disciple Arjuna in the battlefield of Mahabharata. Arjuna wanted to give up the war due to his attachments, but Krishna asked him to rise above his attachments and follow his dharma. Lord Krishna is the ruling deity of Anahata; according to him, our attachments and ego are the only obstacles to spiritual progress.

The vayu associated with this chakra is all prana vayu, which is much more than just the energy of breath: it is the vital life force, as this chakra regulates all the organs of our survival. The seed mantra for this chakra is 'yam', which is also the name of the deity of death in Indian mythology. Another deity associated with the chakra is Hanuman (the monkey-faced god), also known as pawan putra or the 'son of air'. Air is the principle element associated with this chakra. Anahata is the seat of our fears, and people pray to Hanuman to overcome their fears in life.

Anahata is also known to be an important centre for healers to develop compassion. By evolving through this fourth chakra people can master language and poetry and all verbal endeavours to express feelings of the heart, leading to the path of bhakti (devotion). Development of anahata gives you the freedom to escape from a pre-ordained fate and allows you to determine your own destiny.

Imbalances and the tools to heal them

Too many attachments or self-centredness lead to congestion of the heart chakra, which affects lymphatic flow in the axillary and cervical areas and in turn affects the axillary nodes. Blockages of the axillary nodes can lead to breast pain, a fibrocystic breast condition, breast cancer and neck and upper back tightness or pain. This chakra is related to the heart and affects all of its functions: the circulation of blood, the volume of blood, lungs, tension, blood pressure problems, cramps, spasms and sometimes cancer.

In kriya yoga, the practices of uddiyana bandha and kumbhaka are recommended. These pull the abdominal muscles back towards the spine and push the pranas towards the heart. They nourish and strengthen the vibrations of the heart chakra, clearing blockages. Please note that kriya yoga exercises should be done under supervision.

Since the colour of the heart chakra is green, all green crystals such as malachite, green aventurine, green tourmaline, peridot, jade and seraphinite will help. Pink is also associated with love and compassion, and pink stones such as rose quartz, kunzite, morganite and watermelon tourmaline will also assist. Recently, moldavite (a kind of meteorite) has become popular for the heart chakra, as it is considered to be a stone of transformation.

The element associated with the heart chakra is air, which is represented by the leaves of plants. Our favourite essential oil for the heart chakra is tulsi or holy basil, typically a revered plant in India that promotes detachment. This is why the plant is placed outside the house and worshipped. Devotees following krishna consciousness wear tulsi beads, which are made from the stems, and use the beads for chanting. The tulsi plant was the favourite of Lord Krishna since it boosts healing of the heart chakra by promoting detachment. Tulsi leaves are also placed on prasadum (offering to the gods).

The essential oils of peppermint and spearmint are extracted from the leaves and are very useful for all respiratory disorders; they are one of the best remedies for asthma. Other useful leaf oils are eucalyptus and tea tree.

Rose oil has the highest vibrations; some people believe the vibrations of pure rose oil can even reverse breast cancer, though we have not come across any documentary proof of that as yet.

Vishuddhi (throat)

Guna: sattva	
Element: ether	
Vayu: udana	
Auric layer: etheric template body	
Colour: blue	
Structural representation: 16 petals	
Bija mantra: hum	
Developmental age: 28 to 35 years	
Main issues: communication, self-expression	
Gland: thyroid	
Site: hollow of the throat	
Sense: hearing	
Sense organ: ears	
Work organ: mouth	
Animal: elephant	

Deity: five-headed Shiva

Numbers: 5, 7

Planets: Mercury, Ketu

Zodiac signs: Gemini, Virgo

Essential oils: lemon, bergamot, orange, juniper, sandalwood, geranium, cloves

Crystals: angelite, aquamarine, turquoise, cavansite, amazonite, blue calcite, blue lace agate, larimar

The fifth energetic layer, the etheric template body, is associated with the vishuddhi (throat) chakra. This chakra corresponds to the cervical plexus of nerves and controls the thyroid complex and also some systems of articulation, the upper palate and epiglottis.

This chakra governs our communication ability, both verbal and physical. Vishuddhi encompasses the five planes of jnana (awareness), thus bestowing bliss; it's here we receive communications of divine wisdom, allowing us to seek knowledge that is true beyond the limitations of time, cultural conditioning and heredity. Associated with divine will, this chakra is dominant during the ages of 28 to 35, a phase of life during which we seek success in all of our endeavours. Our success is the result of our communication; if we are able communicate well in business and our profession we succeed there, and if we are able communicate well in our personal relationships we make them work successfully. This chakra also regulates our thought expression processes, which are manifested through oratory skills.

The Sanskrit word 'vishuddhi' derives from *shuddhi*, meaning 'to purify'; therefore, this embodies our purification centre. This chakra represents the higher faculty of discrimination and self-expression, and is responsible for receiving or picking up thought vibrations from other people's minds. Any communication received even telepathically can be tested here for correctness and accuracy. Vishuddhi affects all growth and development of the physical body, controlling the thyroid and parathyroid and problems of the throat such as goitre, sore throats, asthma, loss of voice and further suppression of the expression of thoughts.

In traditional symbology, it is represented as a 16-petalled lotus; the 16 petals are also aligned with the nadis associated with this chakra. Each petal of the lotus has the Sanskrit letters 'am', 'aam', 'im', 'eem', 'um', 'oom', 'rim', 'reem', 'lrim', 'lreem', 'em', 'aim', 'om', 'aum', 'am' and 'ah'. In the pericarp of the lotus is a circle that represents the ether element. Within the moon shape of the chakra is the vehicle of the bija, a snow white elephant with a single trunk representing sound and pure consciousness. The seed syllable of the chakra is 'hum'.

The presiding deity depicted is a five-headed Shiva, the five heads representing the five elements in their purest forms. The heads also symbolise the five aspects of Shiva: Aghora, Ishana, Mahadeva, Sada Shiva and Rudra. The shakti depicted is Shakini, an embodiment of purity. The vayu associated with the chakra is udana vayu, which circulates as a vital force throughout the body.

There is a particular nadi (energy channel) associated with the vishuddhi chakra called kurma (tortoise). Once this nadi is activated the practitioner is able to overcome the desire and necessity for food and drink, as the practitioner can connect to the divine fluid secreted from a point at the back of the head called bindu. Therefore, vishudhhi is the legendary fountain of youth, and once activated spontaneous physical rejuvenation can be experienced.

Imbalances and the tools to heal them

Our throat chakra can be affected by all other chakras, as they all are somehow influenced by throat chakra function. For example, the muladhara (base root) chakra is about the physical body and physical stress; when we are in a physical stress situation we are in a fight or flight mode, which impairs our communication.

Most people with thyroid imbalances have sacral or heart chakra blockages as well. Long periods of emotional stress and the inability to express impact our sacral chakra as well as the throat chakra. Blockages of the throat chakra may cause lymphatic congestion in the chin area and sub-mandibular region, besides affecting the lymph nodes in the front and back of the ears, leading to tinnitus (ringing in the ears). An inability to express pain, anguish or trauma affects the heart and throat chakras, impacting axillary, deep cervical and occipital lymph nodes. This could cause problems in the heart, breast, upper back, neck and shoulders.

The manipura (solar plexus) chakra also influences the throat chakra, as this chakra is related to suppressed anger; this causes a heated liver, which could make the body acidic and shows on the face as reddishness or rosacea, especially in the chin area.

This chakra is responsible for the expression of our thoughts and ideas. Sometimes we interact with people who are talking but lose coordination between their thoughts and the expression of those thoughts; in these people the throat and third eye chakras are not coordinated. A well-developed vishuddhi chakra endows exemplary communication and oratory skills, while an imbalance or blockage results in the loss of voice or hoarseness and a fear of being exposed.

The seed mantra associated with the throat chakra is 'hum', which can be chanted in the throat like the sound of a bumble bee. Yoga suggests a mudra known as bhramari mudra, whereby the practitioner uses their fingers to close the eyes and ears while chanting 'hum' like a bumble bee, thus creating an echo in the head. Another bandha or energetic lock to activate the throat chakra is the jalandhara bandha, which is performed by contracting the throat and then folding the chin inwards into the hollow spot between the chest and neck. This cuts off circulation from the head, establishing an independent circuit in the upper part.

Since the chakra is associated with the colour blue, all blue-coloured crystals such as angelite, aquamarine, turquoise, amazonite, blue calcite, blue lace agate, cavansite and larimar are useful for healing and balancing the chakra energies.

The element associated with the throat chakra is ether (or space); the parts of a plant known to represent ether are the fruits. Citrus fruit oils from lemon, bergamot, grapefruit, tangerine and mandarin are useful to balance the chakra energies. They can also be used to clear sore throats, laryngitis and pharyngitis through gargling.

Ajna (third eye)

Guna: sattva
Element: panch mahabhoot (all of the five elements)
Vayu: prana
Auric layer: celestial body
Colours: indigo, white
Structural representation: two petals
Bija mantra: om
Developmental age: not applicable
Main issues: wisdom, intuition, telepathy
Gland: pituitary
Site: between the brows, at the end of the nasal tract
Sense: sixth sense
Sense organ: mind
Work organ: mind
Animal: nada, also known as ardhamatra

Deity: Shiva in the form of Ardhnarishvar

Numbers: 3, 8

Planets: Jupiter, Saturn

Zodiac signs: Sagittarius, Pisces

Essential oils: frankincense, sandalwood, camphor, kewra, rosemary, holy basil, blue lotus, helichrysum

Crystals: azurite, lapis lazuli, sodalite, blue fluorite

Located between the eyebrows is our third eye of conscience. Two physical eyes see the present, while the third gives insight into the future; it is our seat of wisdom and intuition. This chakra is associated with the sixth layer, the celestial body layer, and is connected with celestial love extending beyond the human range of love and encompassing all life forms. It denotes caring and support for the protection and nurturing of all manifested life forms, as represented by the divine one, the brahm.

The word *ajna* derives from a Sanskrit root and means 'to obey' or 'to follow'; it literally means 'command' or refers to the monitoring centre. All experiences and ideas serve only to clarify our perceptions. According to spiritual scriptures this chakra is the seat of guru, and it is here you can discern the communication of the inner guru. It is also called the eye of intuition or divya chakshu, or the gyan netra (eye of knowledge).

Ajna is symbolised as a two-petalled lotus; on the left petal are the letters 'ham' and on the right 'ksham', as the bija mantras of Shiva and Shakti. Within the lotus is a perfect circle symbolising 'shunya' (zero, a void). Within this circle is an inverted triangle representing Shakti, or creativity and manifestation. Above the triangle is the shiva lingam, a symbol of our astral body (an attribute of our personality). Ardhnarishvar (the half male and half female aspects of Shiva and Shakti) stand in the lingam, symbolising the culmination of basic polarity.

Tantra and yoga maintain that the ajna chakra is the command centre and has complete control over our lives. It regulates the functions of the pituitary (the master endocrine gland). Once the chakra is fully cleansed and opened for the first time it presents a state of non-duality, letting go of the ego. In ajna, the yogi themself becomes a divine manifestation, embodying all elements in their purest form or essence.

This chakra is associated with the various cognitive faculties of the mind, both for mental images and abstract idealism. It is also the point of merging of the three nadis: ida, pingala and sushumna. According to Hindu philosophy, these nadis symbolise three holy rivers in India: Ganga (ida), Jamuna (pingala) and Saraswati (sushumna). When the mind is concentrated at this conjunction individual consciousness is transformed, the ego is dissolved and duality ends. As long as there is duality there cannot be samadhi, meaning that as long as there is even a particle of ego further spiritual progress is not possible.

The ajna chakra is also called the guru chakra; this is our guiding principle as it connects us to universal intelligence. When this chakra is open we get correct thoughts, ideas and guidance. This is an essential chakra for developing higher intuition, clairvoyance, abstract thinking and higher mental faculty. Sluggish, dull body activities are a result of a dull third eye chakra. An imbalance results in indecisiveness as an attitude as well as a trait, and a refusal to take responsibility for our actions.

Imbalances and the tools to heal them

We all have different mental capacities, some people being mentally sharp and having thoughts and ideas freely flowing into them, while other people have limited mental capacities. Conditions such ADHD, schizophrenia and bipolar disorders are all the result of a third eye chakra imbalance; these could be genetic or karmic in origin.

Prolonged mental and emotional stress leads to a dull or sluggish third eye chakra, along with confused thinking and fogginess sometimes leading to headaches and migraines. Ajna is also responsible for general allergies to everything, including asthma, and all diseases related to any endocrine gland.

According to Patanjali, all yoga exercises are helpful to relax the mind because yoga is soma-psychic, meaning it is body over mind. While doing a certain yoga exercise we are also practising conscious differential relaxation. When engaged in a yoga pose only a certain part of the body does the exercise, while the rest of the body and mind are relaxed; this is achieved by focusing on the breath. All kinds of breathing exercises also help clear the third eye chakra, as they push more oxygen towards the head. Kapalbhati — the forehead brightener — not only helps the solar plexus area but also the head. Another variation of this exercise is bhastrika, which involves thoracic breathing and pushes more oxygen to the head and stimulates the brain.

The seed mantra for the third eye chakra is 'om', pronounced as 'aum'. If we practise aum chanting at least 21 times daily, keeping focus on the third eye, it will help activate our ajna chakra and facilitate our meditation practice.

The two most popular crystals for ajna are azurite and lapis lazuli. Others that can be used are sodalite, blue fluorite, tanzanite and blue sapphire. Azurite is known as the jewel of wisdom, as some practitioners believe this stone has the ability to transform our grey matter.

Aromatherapy essential oils work on us at the physical, physiological and psychological levels. Essential oils such as holy basil, rosemary, eucalyptus, peppermint and frankincense can stimulate the brain and awaken a dull third eye chakra. The essential oils of sandalwood, blue lotus, clary sage, lavender and kewra help to relax or sedate the mind, thereby reducing mental stress and helping to achieve a meditative state.

Sahasrara (crown)

Guna: trigunatita	
Element: beyond all elements	
Vayu: prana	
Auric layer: causal body	
Colour: gold (for therapy: violet)	
Structural representation: 1000 petals	
Bija mantra: aum	
Developmental age: not applicable	
Main issues: spirituality, beyond self	
Gland: pineal body	
Site: centre of the fontanelle above the head	
Sense: beyond the senses	
Sense organ: none	
Work organ: none	
Animal: not applicable	

Deity: beyond the name and forms; highest consciousness

Number: 8

Planets: Saturn, Ketu

Zodiac sign: Aquarius

Essential oils: brahmi, jatamansi, rosemary, frankincense, holy basil, sage, lotus

Crystals: blue sapphire, amethyst, sugilite, clear quartz

There are two higher centres in the brain that are commonly referred to in kundalini yoga as bindu and sahasrara. Bindu, meaning 'a point', is located at the top back of the head, where Hindu Brahmins keep a tuft of hair. It is also called bindu visarga, which literally means 'falling' or 'drop'; this is represented as a crescent moon and a white drop, which is the nectar dropping down to the vishuddhi chakra. From this point down oneness divides itself into many; it is the seat of nectar or amrit, which feeds our optic system.

From ajna one moves to sahasrara, which is located a little above the fontanelle. Located at the top of the cranium and associated with the cerebral plexus, this chakra is the place of void (emptiness) or sunya (nothingness). This is the plane of tejas (light), the seat of enlightenment, whereby the yogi becomes illuminated just as the sun aura becomes light and radiant. This is depicted as a golden hollow or aura around the pictures and images of ascended masters. In chakra symbology it is depicted as a circle like a full moon, and above this sphere is an umbrella of an inverted 1000-petalled lotus.

Sahasrara is supreme. It is associated with the pineal gland, and is the seat of higher awareness or our connection to universal consciousness. When we are conceived consciousness comes to the child through the crown chakra, then it travels through sushumna nadi all the way down to settle at the muladhara chakra, as our kundalini shakti. Through our spiritual practices we try to raise this consciousness back to the crown chakra so that we can connect and merge with universal consciousness once again.

All of our chakras are within the realms of the psyche. Sahasrara acts through nothing while at the same time acting through everything. It is the centre of super consciousness, where all polarities integrate, thus passing beyond the ever-changing samsara. The opening of this chakra leads to a state of transcendence and hence may be called the attainment of Buddhahood.

Sahasrara is associated with the seventh layer, the ketheric template. Located at the top of the cranium or cerebral plexus, sahasrara synchronises all colours (hence it is white light) and encompasses all senses and their functions; it has all-pervading power. When kundalini is raised up to the sahasrara chakra the yogi becomes realised and the illusion of the individual self is dissolved.

Sahasrara is the culmination of the progressive ascension of kundalini (consciousness) through different chakras. Up to the sixth chakra the yogi may enter a trance in which activity or form still remains within this consciousness; however, in the sahasrara chakra the prana moves upwards and reaches the highest point and the mind establishes itself in a pure void or sunya (zero), the space between the two hemispheres. While meditating the focus should be at the crown chakra, visualising the white light enveloping your body. At this point all activities of the mind — feelings, emotions and desires — are dissolved and the yogi attains a state of true bliss or sat-chit-ananda (truth being bliss). As long as the yogi stays in this physical body he retains non-dual consciousness.

Imbalances and the tools to heal them

The sahasrara chakra is the point of transformation, from the mind/body trap and moving beyond sense consciousness. We live in a sensory world, with sense consciousness perceiving the world and constantly producing uncontrolled thoughts. A person can be a great scientist, artist, thinker, educator or healer, but until the time 'I'-ness is present this chakra will remain blocked. At times there may be a feeling of lightheadedness, a sense of disconnection with the world; this is also a sign of an imbalanced crown chakra and indicates a need to be grounded.

The most important tool for crown chakra healing and balancing is to practise dhyana (meditation); through dhyana we are able to awaken the guru within. Dhyana can be achieved by concentrating on the universal form of God; when this concentration reaches the phase of non-dual consciousness all thoughts and distractions stop and the yogi is able to establish a connection with the higher self. While meditating the focus should be on the top of the head, the seat of the crown chakra.

The best crystals for the crown chakra healing are amethyst, sugilite and clear quartz. When lightheaded or disconnected it is better to use grounding crystals similar to those used for the muladhara (base root) chakra.

In Ayurvedic aromatherapy, when crown chakra balancing and grounding is required we use essential oils representing the earth element such as patchouli, valerian root, angelica root or jatamansi. Other useful oils include brahmi, lavender, holy basil, blue or white lotus, ylang ylang and rosemary.

9

Chakra healing

The holistic approach to health fully acknowledges the integration of mind and body; the well-being of one depends on the good health of the other. Disease is an imbalance of the energies manifesting in the physical body. Chakras are the barometers of our health, and an imbalance of a chakra is an indication of the existence of a disease in any of the organs associated with the imbalanced chakra. Disease first affects our energy body before manifesting in the physical body, therefore we feel out of sorts before we fall sick. Chakra healing is preventative, as we can avoid a potential disease manifesting in the physical body by balancing the chakras.

There are devices and tools that can measure the energy field, take chakra/aura pictures and check chakra health and vibrations through bio-feedback. Energy is universal, and we shape it with our thoughts and feelings. We can help balance the chakras and alter our state of mind using several modalities. Different cultures have a variety of energy healing tools, so we have options available to us for balancing our energies and managing our mental and emotional stress.

Tantra encompasses yoga and Ayurveda. Ayurveda is based on the science of life and longevity using plants and minerals for healing the body, while yoga is described as the union of mind, body and spirit. Ashtanga yoga encompasses eight aspects of life and offers practices to help balance our energies. The principles established in yoga are universal, providing overall development and the evolution of consciousness. Various practices in hatha yoga and pranayama help us become centred and quieten the mind, thereby helping balance chakra energies. There are many other systems of healing that have been developed by different cultures to balance energies.

Chakras respond very well to energy work that is mainly intuitive, and we also have tools such as crystals, aromatherapy essential oils, colour therapy and sound therapy. Some use the term 'alternative therapies', whereas we call them 'complementary therapies' as we can use more than one modality and integrate them to get a desired healing effect. We like to integrate aromatherapy with lymph drainage alongside using crystals and wands. Some of the complementary modalities are explained in this chapter.

Yoga

The basic nature of yoga was well defined in four words by Patanjali in Yoga Sutra 2: Samadhi Pada: *'Yogas chitta-vritti-nirodh'* (yoga is the inhibition of the modifications of the mind).

Yoga has been practised for thousands of years as an effective tool to improve physical, mental and spiritual health. The word 'yoga' is derived from the Sanskrit word *yuj*, meaning to 'unite' or 'join'; it represents the union of the mind, body and spirit and the union of the individual consciousness and cosmic consciousness.

Yoga encompasses the elementary training of the body to promote normal healthy and peaceful human activities. Patanjali called yoga soma-psychic, or mind over body. The aim of yogic discipline is not so

much to cultivate the body for physical strength, quick reflexes or develop muscles but to create a mental make-up through poise, balance and mental endurance. It provides the practitioner with an ability to control the modification of the mind.

Health practitioners today consider the intrinsic health of a human being along with the outer development of the body. The importance of this was realised thousands of years ago by ancient Indian yogis. Yoga and meditation treat a person not merely as a mass of flesh and blood, but as a being with a soul. Health practitioners have come to recognise that the practice of yoga and meditation can provide patients with greater solace and promote better recovery. As soon as a person takes up yoga and meditation their life pattern, personality and diet change. Dr Mimi Guarneri wrote in her book *The Heart Speaks* about the health benefits of integrating an holistic approach to health with yoga, meditation and lifestyle changes to prevent and control cardiovascular diseases. Some of our clients reported great benefits of breathwork, yoga and meditations for their heart conditions, to the extent they could give up traditional medicines.

Yoga helps generate positive, spontaneous energy, and the practitioner attains a balance of mind, body and spirit and is more in control of self. Yogi tend to become puritans (sattvic) and are able to develop willpower to prevent them from smoking, drinking and consuming non-vegetarian food. Yoga is 'a combination of psychoanalysis, psychiatry and physiotherapy', and it directly affects the hypothalamus or the area of the brain that controls endocrine activity.

The practice of yoga has a substantial foundation in science. Yoga asanas (postures) accelerate blood circulation in the body, while pranayama (breath control) abates carbon dioxide content, ensuring better health. There are various types of yoga that incorporate dhyana yoga, bhakti yoga, karma yoga, laya yoga, swar yoga, tantra yoga, hatha yoga and kriya yoga. Out of these, hatha yoga, which involves light physical exercises or postures, is often thought to be the only form of yoga to follow and practise. Patanjali enumerated ashtanga (eight aspects) yoga, involving an eightfold path: yama, niyama, asana, pranayama, pratyahara, dharana, dhyana and samadhi, which are practised for the upliftment of body, mind and spirit.

Yama concerns the rules to be followed by the practitioner living in a society. As a social being living in a society we need to follow the rules of the society and live consciously. All religions came into existence for the same reason: to give the followers of the religion certain guidance to a way of life and to set rules for living harmoniously that involve non-violence, honesty, truthfulness, kindness and forbearance.

Niyama, a set program commensurate with self-discipline, is adopted by the practitioner for personal development. The program involves austerity, contentment, charity and worshipping or following certain spiritual practices. To stay healthy a certain amount of self-discipline is important; a lack of self-discipline will lead to all kinds of health problems.

Asana means a 'steady and relaxing posture'. Asana involves light physical exercises designed to achieve a certain level of physical agility and flexibility. Hatha yoga prescribes 84 asanas (postures) to help tune up the physical body, out of which only a certain few need to be practised; these are prescribed according to our physical needs.

The practise of asanas helps the flexiblity and mobility of muscles and joints, relieving niggling aches and pains. Yoga asanas also help to control the mind and mental stress. Light yoga exercises and observation of the breath promote conscious differential relaxation; during a yoga exercise only certain muscles or parts of the body are involved while the mind and the rest of the body are relaxed. This is achieved by keeping focus on the breath, which helps control mental diversion and reduce mental and/or emotional stress.

Pranayama means 'control of pranas', which flow through our breath. Pranas are the vehicle of the mind and nourish our consciousness. According to tantra our lives are not measured in the number of years, months and days but in the number of breaths we take, so if we breathe fast we die young so the key is to breathe deeply and slowly.

Pranayama involves the manipulation of breathing patterns to move pranas in certain directions. It entails regulating the period between inhalation and exhalation, and also disciplining the complete respiratory process. In pranayama the inhalation is called 'puraka', holding the breath in is called 'kumbhaka' and the exhalation is called 'rechaka'. This kind of breathing practice combined with yoga postures and bandhas is a part of kriya yoga. An important and useful pranayama exercise that can be practised daily is anulom vilom, or alternate nostril breathing. This helps balance the pranas in the ida and pingala nadis, restoring mental and emotional balance.

Pratyahara means 'withdrawal of senses'. We experience this world through our five senses of sight (eyes), touch (skin), taste (tongue), hearing (ears) and smell (nose); these are the doors of the mind, connecting it to the outer world. As long as our senses are engaged in the outside world it is difficult to turn inwards; to do this we need to withdraw our senses by focusing on the breath. It requires constant practice to bring about the internalisation of the mind and control the senses.

Dharana means 'fixation of the mind on an object'. The mind is restless and keeps drifting from object to object; to control this distraction we need to direct it to a single object. In chakra meditation we try to focus the mind on various chakra points from muladhara upwards, each chakra becoming a point of focus. This is practised while chanting the seed syllables associated with each chakra and directing breath energy to the chakra point. By the time our focus reaches the crown chakra mental diversion ceases, paving the way for meditation.

Dhyana means 'meditation', which is training the mind into a state of thoughtlessness. Through chakra chanting and meditation, while focusing on each chakra from muladhara up to sahasrara we move our awareness through each chakra. By the time our awareness reaches the crown chakra our mental diversion stops.

Dhyana (meditation) happens when mental diversion stops, leading to the final state, which is called **samadhi**. Samadhi is the state of equilibrium, a higher awareness, where individual consciousness is able to merge with the higher consciousness, leading to self-realisation of Aham Brahmasmi: I am the spirit Soul. It is a state of complete bliss.

Out of the aforesaid eight aspects, yama, niyama, asana and pranayama are clubbed together as bahiranga (or external) yoga and are generally practised for physical and mental health. Dharana, dhyana and samadhi form the antaranga (internal) yoga, also called raja yoga, while pratyahara (withdrawal of the senses) is considered to be a bridge between the two. Certain hatha yoga exercises combined with pranayama and raja yoga are used as tools of kundalini awakening and are grouped together by various teachers as a part of kundalini yoga.

Kriya yoga incorporates practices from hatha yoga, pranayama and dhyana besides practices of mudras and bandhas to transform the inner core. An action outwards is called karma, but kriya yoga practices are actions inwards to move the pranas, the vehicles of our consciousness. There is a certain set of kriya yoga practices designed for chakra healing and balancing that should only be practised under the supervision of a trained teacher.

Mudras

A 'mudra', meaning 'seal', is a body and finger posture. Mudras have been used for thousands of years in Indian spiritual and tantric practices to seal the prana. It is a process of gaining control of the life force to restore the balance of energies. Hatha yoga terms some of its facial exercises as mudras, such as bhramari mudra, simha mudra and brahma mudra. Even in classic Indian dances, dancers use hand mudras along with body language.

It is an ancient discipline to rejuvenate the body, mind and spirit. Acupressure and reflexology also believe that the palms and the soles of the feet have nerve endings connected to a large part of the brain associated with our organs and glands. By touching and pressing these points a cerebral activity can be initiated through energy meridians to release the energy blocks.

According to Ayurveda, most physical ailments are due to imbalances of the five body elements. In mudra yoga we try to achieve an equilibrium of the basic elements of earth, water, fire, air and ether by using the

Gyan mudra

Apan mudra

Prithvi mudra

Varun mudra

Surya mudra

Prana mudra

Abhaya mudra

Shunya mudra

fingers of our hands in a scientific manner to realign the energies. Some mudras are extremely useful for meditation and promote a state of deep concentration and stillness of the mind. Various mudras such as gyan mudra, jal (water) mudra, prana (life energy) mudra, prithvi (earth) mudra, varun mudra, vayu (air) mudra, apan mudra, shunya (space) mudra and sun mudra are used for balancing body elements to heal the corresponding chakras.

Gyan mudra is one of the most important and widely accepted in yoga and meditational practices. To attain this, join the tip of the forefinger and the tip of the thumb. To get the maximum benefits, hold together gently for 15 to 30 minutes.

Benefits: purifies the mind of the practitioner, improving intelligence and wisdom. It helps to lift mood and relieve insomnia and depression, providing a feeling of joy. It helps people with addiction to intoxicants and drug.

Apan mudra: joining the tips of the middle and ring fingers with the tip of the thumb forms the apan mudra. This mudra is associated with the muladhara chakra and regulates apana vayu.

Benefits: cleanses and purifies the body, facilitating the discharge of waste material (urination and menstruation) from the body, releasing negative energy. This is a very useful mudra for people who feel lethargic.

Prithvi mudra: this mudra helps to increase the earth element, hence activating the root chakra. It is useful for people who want to gain weight. To attain the mudra, touch the ring finger at the tip of the thumb and press gently. The remaining three fingers should be held straight, with the palms at the knees. Practise for 15 to 20 minutes.

Benefits: this mudra cures weakness of the body and mind, increasing life force and giving vigour to an ailing person. It helps with grounding, boosts self-confidence and gives peace of mind.

Varun mudra: to attain this mudra, join the tips of the little fingers and the thumbs and keep the remaining three fingers straight. Keep the hands at the folded knees, and keep the palm tight while the rest of the hand should be relaxed. Practise for 10 to 15 minutes daily.

Benefits: helps improve circulation and skin quality and prevents dehydration and urinary problems. It is a suitable mudra for the swadhisthana (sacral) chakra and associated imbalances.

Surya mudra: join the tips of both ring fingers at the root of both thumbs. Allow the other three fingers of each hand to remain straight. Keep the hands at the folded knees, with the palms facing up. Put a little pressure in the palm; the rest of the hand should be relaxed. This mudra is useful for the manipura (solar plexus) chakra. It should be practised for 10 to 15 minutes daily.

Benefits: generates body heat and aids digestion and weight control. It also relieves health problems such as diabetes and regulates cholesterol and liver imbalances.

Prana mudra: this is formed by joining the tips of the ring finger and little finger with the tip of the thumb. It balances all vayus in the body and is recommended for the anahata (heart) chakra and all chakras above that.

Benefits: energises the heart, improves the functioning of the lungs and eyesight and revitalises the body.

Abhaya mudra: this is normally practised after reciting the gayatri mantra. As with the gyan mudra, touch the forefinger to the tip of the thumb and raise the hands vertically to the side of your head. This mudra is useful for anxiety-prone and fearful people, and helps to balance both the solar plexus and heart chakras.

Benefits: the mind becomes fearless, giving a feeling of courage and strength.

Shunya mudra: this mudra is attained by putting the middle finger of both hands at the root of the thumb and pressing gently. Keep the hands on or near the knees with the palms facing up; maintain the position for 5 to 10 minutes. This mudra regulates the space element and is thus useful for the throat chakra and those above it.

Benefits: strengthens the heart and gum muscles, and relieves toothache and earache. It also regulates thyroid gland functions and helps with deafness and vertigo.

Mudras can be practised while seated, lying down, standing or even walking. However, please ensure that the body posture is symmetrical and centred. Its sounds easy but can be difficult sometimes when our fingers are inflexible and rebellious and holding a position for 10 to 15 minutes becomes tedious. Normally a mudra should be practised for a minimum of 10 to 15 minutes to have an effect; for a therapeutic effect a mudra should be practised for up to 45 minutes. You can also perform mudras three times a day for 10 to 15 minutes each time.

Meditation

Meditation (dhyana) is the integral part of antaranga (internal) yoga. It is an effective tool to achieve a balance of mind, body and spirit. According to Patanjali, dhyana is the state where mental diversion stops and there is nothing on which to focus except a continuous flow of awareness, allowing the practitioner to connect with the higher consciousness.

Meditation does not mean merely contemplation; it originates from the Latin word *mederi*, meaning 'to heal'. It is intended to heal mental afflictions caused by psychological stress. Various teachers promote meditation in different forms, but the ultimate objective is the same: achieving a tranquil state of mind devoid of thoughts and connection to universal consciousness. It may not be easy to achieve a state of thoughtlessness as the mind drifts constantly. However, certain practices such as chakra meditation help to steady the state of the mind by initially focusing attention on each chakra point while chanting the chakra seed syllable and ultimately moving consciousness to the crown chakra, staying connected there until there are no thoughts.

The benefits of meditation include a greater sense of relaxation in both mind and body, greater flexibility of thinking and an ability to meet a situation with freshness and insight. From the standpoint of pure physical expression, it can help loosen the knots and tensions trapped in the body by dissipating emotions. It can help to change both facial expression and body posture, thereby softening and strengthening at the same time. These are some of the possible results, but they are not the goals. Meditation helps strengthen the positive qualities of compassion, patience and wisdom and free us of conflicting emotions and erroneous beliefs.

Chanting

Chanting, or japa, destroys sins and liberates a person from the cycles of birth and death. Japa is repetition of a particular letter, word, mantra or sentence; 'naam japa' is repetition or chanting of a deity's name; and 'mantra japa' refers to the repetition of a particular mantra. This path of spiritual practice is known as nama sankirtan yoga (path of chanting the Lord's name).

Our subconscious mind carries millions of impressions that arise out of our prakruti (nature). The mind, intellect and subconscious mind (chitta) are the constituents of prakruti, and they all function according to their own characteristics and create their own impressions. When we do any repetitive activity it sedates the mind and prevents its vriti (modification).

Ancient sages used to proscribe a guru mantra to their followers that was appropriate for each one in order to balance their chakras, as they had the ability to see the aura and understand the chakra imbalances. This is still practised by some sages.

Chanting can be done by people of all religions and hues as per their faith and beliefs. Chanting the name of our ishta (favourite) deity or angel also helps to balance energies. There is so much information available now on mantras and chanting. The market is flooded with audio tapes and CDs of the mantra chanting; however, it is very important to understand the energy and effect of the mantras before you chant them.

One of the most powerful mantras is the gayatri mantra:

'Om bhur bhuva swaha, tat savitur varenyam,

Bhargo devasya dhimahi, dhiyo yona prachodayat.'

This potent mantra helps clear negative energies and even entities. It invokes the energy of the sun (the fire element) and should be chanted with care, preferably in the early morning or late evening and in the presence of water. The best way to chant it is to do a minimum of three japa malas (of 108 beads). Prayer beads are recommended, as chanting generates positive vibrations that stay with the beads.

Most prayer beads consist of either 27, 54 or 108 beads, which all add up to 9: the number of completion.

Bija mantras associated with each of the chakras are easy to understand and follow; they are short and simple to remember. Aum chanting is the best to use for chanting. When you focus on a chakra point while aum chanting you will be able to feel the vibrations generated every time you repeat the syllable.

Chanting the names or mantras of the deities associated with each chakra is a common practice in Hindu culture. All deities have their own energy vibrations, and by chanting and praying to the deities we invoke the energy of that deity.

For the **muladhara (base root)** chakra, for which the ruling deity is Ganesha, we can chant:

'*Om shri ganeshaya namah*' or '*Om shri gan ganpathaye namh*'.

The **swadhisthana (sacral)** chakra is considered to be the centre for procreation and the seat of kundalini shakti. The Sanskrit word *kula* means 'family''; kuldevi is the form of Shakti, the benefactor of the family, while kuldevata also represents the benefactor energy of the family deity. Chanting the name of the family deity or simply 'kuldevi' will benefit the family and remove any curse on it. A curse on the family can be recognised when all family members are suffering from any kind of physical, mental or emotional affliction or financial problem.

The chanting mantra for swadhisthana is:

'*Shri kul deviyah namh*' or '*Shri kul devtayeh namh*'.

Alternatively, you can chant the name of shakti durga:

'*Om shri durga deviyahe namh.*'

For the **manipura (solar plexus)** chakra the seed mantra is '*ram*', which is the name of the deity Shri Ram. Chanting his name helps strengthen the solar plexus chakra:

'*Om shri ram, jai ram, jai jai ram.*'

Alternatively, chant the gayatri mantra, as it invokes sun energy.

Lord Krishna is an avatar (reincarnation) of Lord Vishnu, sustainer of the universe; chanting his name helps the **anahata (heart)** chakra, providing detachment, healing and courage:

'*Om namho bahgwate vasudevayah.*'

For the **vishuddhi (throat)** chakra the seed mantra is 'humm'; chanting the following hanuman mantra will help to generate the same vibrations, develop courage and clear any throat chakra blockages:

'*Hung hanumate namh.*'

The **ajna (third eye)** chakra is the seat of guru, the guiding principle. By chanting the following mantra we can invoke our guiding principle and get mental clarity:

'*Shri guruvey namh.*'

Alternatively, you can chant the name of '*Shri gurudev datt*'.

Dattatrey is an incarnation of the divine trinity of Brahma, Vishnu and Shiva. Chanting this mantra will connect us to the energy of supreme consciousness.

For the **sahasrara (crown)** chakra the chanting of any of the following mantras is useful:

'*Om namo shivaya*' or '*Shivom*' or '*Om soham*'.

Whenever a japa mala or rosary is used for chanting, certain guidelines need to be followed to get the maximum benefit of the practice:

- Don't cross the merumani, the central bead. When you reach the central bead during chanting, instead of continuing and crossing past it reverse the japa mala so that you begin from the first bead again. The objective of this spiritual practice is to maintain the balance in our sushumna nadi. If you carry on in one direction you activate either of the other nadis, ida or pingala.

- The beads of the mala should be drawn towards yourself. The prana vayu is active when the beads are drawn towards you and samana vayu is active when you turn them away; we feel better vibrations when we are drawing the mala or rosary towards our own self.

The mere mechanical pronunciation of mantras is not deemed to be chanting. A seeker should become endowed with divine emotions and awareness of the Lord's omnipotence. Chanting with the correct pronunciation will help to generate divine energy. You can also weave the chant in your breath, then you don't have to say it out loud. For example, inhale while saying 'om', hold the breath while chanting 'shri' and chant 'guru dev dutt' while releasing the breath.

This kind of chanting done with devotion invokes the bhavana of the mantra. When a substance is repeatedly dipped in a solution it gets fully immersed into it; thus a seeker should chant regularly with devotion and get fully engrossed into it, merging with the mantra. This is the prime objective of chanting.

Sound

Nada, or sound and music, is the manifestation of sound in harmony. The Big Bang is believed to be the precursor for the beginning of the universe and life on it. In Indian scripture 'om' or 'omkara' is not a word but the primordial sound made before the beginning of all manifested things on Earth. This is supported by the biblical reference to the Word, which existed before anything else. The word 'universe' itself connotes the 'single rhythm in which the world is nurtured as a verse'.

The idea that sound affects our health is not a new one. Sound is resonance, the frequency at which an object naturally vibrates; it is the representation of energy vibrations and has the ability to alter the state of consciousness. Sound has a physiological effect on us as its vibrations are not merely heard but also felt. The resonance can lower the heart rate, relax brain wave patterns and promote meditation and sleep.

Mystics and sages of ancient cultures were aware of the effect music could have on harmonising, balancing and healing human energy. Chanting and recitation of mantras is a part of the Indian spiritual practices of bhakti yoga. Music is a kind of sadhana (spiritual practice) and was practised by gandharvas (a group of celestial musician). Bhakti yoga has two aspects: music created with devotion to the Lord, and devotional songs. In India, Meera Bai, the singing saint, has been the symbol of devotion to Lord Krishna through her melodious bhajans, or songs in praise of the Lord. People associated with krishna consciousness are engrossed in the energy of krishna while chanting '*Hare rama hare Krishna, Krishna Krishna, hare hare.*'

Viththal is another name and form of the deity Sri Krishna, whose temple is in the small town of Pandharpur in Maharashtra, India. A recent research study was carried out by an institute in Pune to investigate the health benefits of chanting the name 'Viththal Viththal'. The study used 25 people with various health problems who were asked to chant 'Viththal Viththal' in a quiet place for at least 10 minutes every day for 15 days. All of the subjects showed a marked improvement, especially the ones with heart conditions such as high blood pressure and erratic palpitation, or arterial fibrillation.

The study concluded that during the chanting the letters 'ththa' vibrate your heart to a certain frequency, which helps heart health.

There have been many saints and seekers all over the world who have used music and devotional songs as the path to connect to supreme consciousness. Music and devotional songs do incorporate mantras, specifically bija mantras, but they are more than an extension of the repeated chanting of the mantras. Music is a vital energy that penetrates all forms of manifestations. We can use it to attain unity with the life forces and to connect to the innermost core of all things.

The ragas (melodies on the Indian music scale) and the notes of music can create different effects on different people. They can have a calming and relaxing effect, as they bring about a balance of emotions and energy, and they can be stimulating and uplifting. In ancient India Tansen was the musician in the court of Akbar, the great Mogul emperor; whenever he used to play raga deepika (lamp) at dusk the sound vibrations would light up all the lamps in the palace.

Practitioners of sound healing, also called sounders, use singing bowls and tuning forks. Sound from Tibetan singing bowls train the brain to move into theta brainwave frequencies, which induce deep meditative and peaceful states, clarity of mind and intuition. The sound creates resonance, the frequency at which an object naturally vibrates. The sound vibrations impact the nervous system by promoting relaxation, which inhibits the stress or pain response.

Through the use of the human voice and tools such as singing bowls or tuning forks that resonate to stimulate healing, sound therapy has become one of a growing number of subtle-energy therapies that make up the field of vibrational medicine.

Different musicians and practitioners have used their abilities in the area of vibrational medicine. Like the bija mantras for each of the chakras, Western music practitioners use specific tones and keys for each of the chakras. For example:

- deep C and C major for muladhara
- D and D major for swadhisthana
- E and E major for manipura
- F and F major for anahata
- G and G major for vishuddhi
- A and A major for ajna
- H and H major for sahasrara.

Aromatherapy

Each of us has an individual and unique sense of smell, which is one of the most powerful and instinctive of all our senses. For aeons we have relied on it for our choice of food, medicinal herbs, to sense the dangers of warand for religious/spiritual purposes and sex. We continue to use aromas to communicate our personalities and emotions through the perfumes we use and the gifts we give. When we take flowers to someone in hospital we are using a simple form of aromatherapy and colour energy to help the patient feel better. The bouquet contains essential oils that give its smell, helping to lift spirits. Aromatherapy is the modern term for using plant essential oils to improve physical and mental well-being.

In the Indian epic story Ramayana there is an anecdote wherein Laxmana, the younger brother of Shri Ram, lost consciousness when he was hit by an arrow. He was revived by the vaidya (Ayurvedic practitioner) through inhalation of an extract of sanjeevani booti (a herb found abundantly in the Himalayas).

Dhanwantari, the deity associated with the Indian healing tradition of Ayurveda, is considered to be the param vaidya (supreme healer). According to him we use medicine in three forms, in ascending order of efficacy: in solid form as vatis (tablets) or churan (powder); in liquid form as syrups or tisanes; and in gaseous form. The latter is the plant essential oils as they evaporate when exposed to air; this is considered to be the most potent form of the medicine.

Plant essential oils

Used as a form of medicine through the ages, essential oils are the volatile extracts of the plant, their pranas or life force; they are the most gentle of gifts from nature to us. They are extracted from different parts of the plant such as flowers, leaves, seeds, bark, wood, roots and even gum resins. The most potent representation of the plant's therapeutic and healing properties, they are highly aromatic and have a balancing effect on our mind, body and emotions through inhalations and topical application to the body.

Various researches have shown that essential oils have the highest frequency of any natural substance known to man, creating an environment in which disease, bacteria, viruses and funguses cannot live. We believe that the chemistry and frequencies of essential oils have the ability to help us maintain the optimal frequency wherein disease cannot exist.

Essential oils work on us at different levels, physical, physiological and psychological, besides working at the vibrational level. For chakra healing we look for essential oils that resonate with frequency of the elements associated with the chakras. What human beings are to the animal world, herbs are to the plant kingdom. The three gunas and five elements present in us also have their representation in the plant world: the roots, trunk and branches with their leaves and flowering tops represent the three gunas.

Earth: plant roots are associated with the earth element. Essential oils from the roots of a plant resonate with the vibrations of the muladhara (base root) chakra and have the ability to energise and balance the chakra. Among the preferred essential oils, jatamansi (Indian spikenard) is known for its use by Mary Magdalene to massage Jesus Christ's feet before the last supper. Other useful oils for muladhara are angelica root, valerian root, costus root, nagarmotha, patchouli and vetiver.

Water: a plant's stem and trunk work as the waterways for the entire plant, thus they are associated with the water element. The essential oils extracted from them are useful for healing and balancing the swadhisthana (sacral) chakra, in particular sandalwood, cedarwood, ginger, juniper berry, clary sage and jasmine.

Fire: the manipura (solar plexus) chakra is associated with the fire element, which in plants is represented by the flowers and spices. Brightly coloured flowers and spices such as black pepper and clove provide useful oils to energise and balance the solar plexus chakra. Other useful oils are rosemary, marjoram, chamomile, lavender, thyme, fennel seed, cardamom, garlic and black seed (kalonji).

Air: the air element is associated with the anahata (heart) chakra. As plants breathe through their leaves, it is represented in the leaves of a plant. The most revered and useful plant for the heart chakra is holy basil (tulsi), the oil of which promotes detachment and helps with respiratory disorders. Other useful essential oils are peppermint, eucalyptus, tea tree, lemongrass, rosemary, frankincense and lavender.

Ether: known also as space or akasha tattva, the ether element is associated with the vishuddhi (throat) chakra. In plants this element is associated with the fruits and the seeds. The useful oils are lemon, orange, bergamot, bayberry, sandalwood, lotus and tea tree.

The ajna (third eye) chakra controls panch mahabhoot (all five elements); we can use any of the sattvic essential oils for the third eye chakra. Essential oils such as holy basil, rosemary, eucalyptus, peppermint and frankincense can stimulate the brain and activate a dull third eye chakra. The essential oils of sandalwood, blue lotus, clary sage, lavender and kewra help relax or sedate the mind, thereby reducing mental stress and helping to achieve a meditative state.

Since essential oils are highly concentrated, it is recommended they are diluted in a suitable base oil before applying to the skin. Lotus seed, jojoba or black sesame seed (til) oil can be used as a base for chakra anointments. From an efficacy view point, it has been demonstrated through different testing methods such as aura pictures or the biofeedback method that essential oils used for chakra healing show instantaneous results on chakra vibrations. Not only do essential oils help to balance chakras; they also help to balance physiological symptoms associated with chakra imbalances.

For self-application, chakra anointments should be used on the front of the body. When applying to someone else, it is best if they are applied at the back. Chakra anointments can also be used in conjunction with crystals and crystal wands.

Chakra anointment

Though the chakras are anatomically undetectable, they are linked to different systems of our body. Since each of the chakras controls certain organs and glands, the imbalance may result in physical, physiological or psychological disorders. Chakra anointments prepared with natural essential oils accelerate the process of harmonising and balancing the chakras, along with helping to heal diseases in the associated organs or glands.

Always use the right hand middle finger for the application of chakra oils on the front of the body, and apply in a clockwise (right to left) motion (visualise yourself being the clock). Start with three slow rotations; you can do more if you intuitively feel the need. Follow the same sequence every time you use the chakra oils, making sure to wipe your hand with a tissue after using each oil.

Chakra work should begin with the ajna (third eye) chakra, as physiologically it is associated with the pituitary gland, which influences and controls the functioning of all other glands. Spiritually it is associated with our guru, the guiding principle.

First, a drop of ajna chakra oil blend should be applied at the third eye point between the eyebrows; you can use the middle or ring finger of your right hand to apply the oil. Gently rub three to five times in a clockwise direction.

Next, using the middle finger apply a drop of muladhara (base root) chakra oil blend at the coccyx area, gently rubbing in a circular motion for three to five cycles.

Next, apply the swadhisthana (sacral) chakra oil just above the pubic area. Use one to two drops only, again in a clockwise direction. As this is a wider area you can use the flat side of a couple of your fingers and rub for three to five cycles.

Next, for the manipura (solar plexus) chakra, put two to three drops of the oil blend on a couple of fingers and apply under the V of the ribcage, located below the diaphragm. Massage gently three to five times at the solar plexus area while you breathe in through the abdomen.

For the anahata (heart) chakra, located at the sternum right at the centre of the chest, use one to two drops of the oil blend on the fingertips and rub in a clockwise direction.

For the vishuddhi (throat) chakra, apply the oil blend on a couple of fingers at the centre of the throat, rubbing clockwise. Tap the area of the throat gently, as it helps to activate the thyroid gland.

For the sahasrara (crown) chakra, located at the fontanelle or top of the head, use the palm of your hand to apply a drop of the chakra oil. Close your eyes, and take your awareness to the chakra point.

Once you have completed the process of chakra anointment we are ready for the meditation.

Chakra dhyana

The objective of the chakra dhyana is to balance our chakras for optimum health. Dhyana meditation:

- improves concentration by controlling mental diversion
- helps to reduce mental and emotional stress
- balances our chakra energies, promoting health
- increases self-awareness through regular practice
- promotes cardiovascular and immune health.

Make yourself comfortable in a meditative posture (asana), preferably the siddhasana or lotus pose, on the ground or otherwise on a chair. Follow this procedure:

- Place both hands on your knees with the palms facing upwards and the thumbs and forefingers together.
- Close your eyes and make your body steady throughout, keeping the spinal column upright and straight while your back and shoulders are fully relaxed.
- The whole body should be relaxed and immobile, maintaining absolute awareness of the physical body for few minutes.
- Become aware of your spinal column, which should be erect.

- Bring your awareness to the ajna (third eye) chakra, which is located inside the brain at a point directly behind the centre of your eyebrows.

- Observe your breath for a few moments, focusing it at the third eye chakra point.

- Take a deep breath and start chanting 'aum' while releasing your breath. Synchronise the chanting of 'aum' with pulsation at the ajna chakra. Maintain this awareness of the pulsation for some time.

- Repeat three times.

- Shift your awareness to the muladhara (base root) chakra, located at the perineum (between the genitals and the anus).

- Focusing at that chakra point, contract your anal genital muscles up to your lower abdomen. As in the practice of mula bandha, hold the contraction for a while and repeat three times.

- Start chanting the seed mantra for muladhara — 'la . . . am' — with each inhalation. Start with 'la' and go on, prolonging the 'aaaaaa . . . m'.

- Keep your focus on the chakra point in order to feel the breath vibrations travelling all the way to muladhara.

- Repeat the chanting three times.

- Shift your awareness to the swadhisthana (sacral) chakra, in the region of the tailbone at the back and the pubic region at the front.

- Keeping your focus in the area, begin to contract and relax your genitals (vajroli mudra). Contract, hold the count for three to five, then release. Repeat three times.

- Chant 'va . . . am', the seed mantra for swadhisthana, prolonging the 'aaaaaa . . . m'.

- Feel the vibrations of your breath reaching the chakra point, keeping your focus there. You will be able to feel the breath vibrations travelling along with the chant to the chakra point.

- Repeat three times.

- Shift your awareness to your abdominal region. The manipura (solar plexus) chakra point is located in the hollow or V of your ribcage approximately 10 cm above the navel.

- Contract your anal muscles along with your abdominal muscles, holding for a few seconds then releasing. Repeat three times.

- Making sure to keep your focus at the chakra point, start chanting 'ra . . . am' (the seed mantra for manipura), again prolonging the 'aaaaaa . . . m'.

- Repeat three times.

- Bring your awareness to the centre of your chest at the anahata (heart) chakra point.

- Feel the space in your chest and lungs filling up by contracting and expanding with the rhythm of your natural spontaneous breath.

- Hold your breath in your chest and release from your mouth.

- Repeat three times.

- Chant 'ya . . . am' (the seed mantra for the heart chakra), again prolonging the 'aaaaaa . . . m'.

- Repeat three times.

- Feel the vibrations in the heart chakra; if you focus on your heart you should be able to listen to your own heart beats.

- Bring your awareness to the throat pit and then take it directly back to your neck at the vishuddhi chakra point.

- Feel each breath passing through your throat.

- Hum the seed mantra for vishuddhi: 'hum'. Start chanting 'hummmmm', then close your mouth and let the sound ring in the throat like the sound of a bumble bee.

- Feel the pulsations in the throat chakra and the resonance of your humming sound inside your head.

- Repeat three times.

- Move your attention to the sahasrara (crown) chakra at the top of your head.

- Begin the crown chakra seed mantra of 'aum' and, keeping your focus on your coccyx, start chanting and allowing the vibrations of your prolonged 'aaa . . . au . . . m' chanting to move through your spine to the top of your head.

- Repeat this three to seven times, keeping your focus and awareness on the crown chakra. This is the point of our connection with supreme consciousness and the beginning of our meditation.

- Stay connected as long as possible.

- Visualise the white light showering on you, and feel the tranquillity flowing through.

Before opening your eyes, rub your hands together gently then rub them over your eyes, face and head. This will nourish you with cosmic vibrations received during the meditation.

Crystals

Crystals have been used for aeons for healing and balancing the body, mind and spirit and to re-establish broken links between them. Crystal healing is considered to be a complementary therapy whereby the healer uses the crystal energy to enhance the healing processes of the being on which it is being used. Each crystalline form has its own individual energy and its own personality. As mineralogical structures crystals contain more than one mineral, possessing a melding of the energies of the minerals they contain. Each crystal can be used in unique ways to assist a person to understand the multifaceted nature of their existence on Earth. Crystals have been used to act as catalysts for healing and to assist a person to become reunited with source.

Chakras, the energy centres of our bodies, reflect our physical, mental, emotional and spiritual energy. We can heal and balance these vibrations simply by using crystals that resonate with the particular chakra's colour. It's a form of vibrational medicine, with the crystals having a healing and balancing effect on the chakra's vibrations. Therapists using various forms of healing can combine crystals to enhance and accelerate healing processes. For example, a reiki or pranic healer can use crystals or crystal wands during the healing process. Quartz and its varieties such as amethyst, rose quartz and smoky quartz are the most commonly used crystals for healing purpose.

Crystals for the muladhara (base root) chakra

This chakra is aligned with our etheric body and also with automatic and autonomic functions, since it is associated with physical functioning and sensation or feelings of pain and pleasure. Muladhara is the first chakra in the spiritual evolution of humankind, where we go beyond animal consciousness and start to be a real human being. This chakra is associated with the earth element and has the densest vibrations, which show up as red in colour. It stresses the importance of being grounded in the here and now.

Its ruling planet is Mars, and the most useful crystals for this chakra are red coral, red jasper, haematite, black onyx, black tourmaline and black brown or moss agates. Some healers also use smoky quartz for healing of this chakra. Clearing a blockage in this area requires the visualisation of healing vibrations and light entering the body, with the crystal either directed towards the area or placed on the chakra location. It is recommended that the muladhara chakra is balanced in conjunction with the crown chakra.

Crystals for the swadhisthana (sacral) chakra

This chakra is associated with our emotional body; it denotes the desire centre of our being. Desires for physical sensations and material things play at a person's mind, making them restless and confused. This chakra is related to procreation, material achievements and power-seeking attitudes and behaviour. It controls the unconscious in human beings. The main reason for blockages here are emotional imbalances, which result in malfunctions in the circulatory and the excretory systems of the body and affect lymphatic flow, resulting in problems associated with body fluids and all the organs related to their production.

The crystals suitable for this chakra are carnelian, hessonite garnet, orange jasper and orange or honey calcite. Moonstone, pearl and mother of pearl also help with emotional balance. Clearing this chakra involves circling the area in a clockwise direction with the crystal pointed towards it slightly. Visualisation of a light coming through the stone to this point is important. You can also use one or more crystals and place them over the chakra area.

Citrine

Crystals for the manipura (solar plexus) chakra

This chakra is associated with our mental body. It corresponds to the solar plexus, which is the seat of anxieties, and controls the entire process of digestion, assimilation and temperature regulation at the physical level. A person dominated by the third chakra will strive for personal power and recognition, even if it is to the detriment of relationships with family and friends. Located under the V of the ribcage a few centimetres above the navel, this chakra represents the fire element and is associated with the colour yellow; it is ruled by the sun.

The crystals suitable for this chakra are all of the yellow crystals such as citrine, tiger's eye, pyrite, yellow calcite and yellow sapphire; these will help to activate the solar plexus chakra. If your solar plexus is already overactive then do not wear yellow, as it can aggravate the symptoms related to overactivity of the solar plexus such as acid reflux, headaches, migraines and hypertension. In that condition you need the cooling energy of green-coloured crystals such as those used for the heart chakra.

Malachite

Crystals for the anahata (heart) chakra

Our fourth layer or astral body, along with the very special heart chakra, is associated with unconditional acceptance, love for ourselves and all that forms the universe. Located at the centre of chest, this chakra is associated with the air element and the colour green; it is influenced by the planets Mercury and Venus. It is also an important centre for healers to develop compassion.

Since the colour of the heart chakra is green, all green crystals such as malachite, green aventurine, green tourmaline, peridot, jade, seraphinite and moldavite will help. However, pink is also associated with love and this chakra is considered to be the seat of love and compassion, thus pink stones such as rose quartz, kunzite, morganite and watermelon tourmaline will also help.

Crystals for the vishuddhi (throat) chakra

The fifth layer or etheric template body, along with the vishuddhi chakra, is associated with the higher will in association with the divine will. This chakra corresponds to the cervical plexus of nerves and controls the thyroid complex. It controls some systems of articulation, the upper palate and epiglottis and aligns with the element ether and the colour blue. This chakra represents communication, power and self-expression.

This chakra benefits from all the blue-coloured crystals such as aquamarine, angelite, blue topaz, blue lace agate, moonstone, amazonite, blue calcite, cavansite, larimar and turquoise. Hold the crystal a few centimetres away from the chakra or place the stone near the chakra point.

Crystals for the ajna (third eye) chakra

Ajna denotes caring and support for the protection and nurturing of all manifested life forms. It is associated with the sixth layer or celestial body and is located between the brows. This chakra is associated with our sixth sense, the colour indigo and the planets Jupiter and Saturn.

All deep blue-coloured crystals are useful for this chakra, such as azurite, lapis lazuli, sodalite, purple fluorite and even clear quartz. You can either place the crystal at the chakra point or use clear quartz to heal and energise the chakra. To clear any blockages in this area, hold the crystal a few centimetres away from the chakra point and visualise the white light passing through.

Crystals for the sahasrara (crown) chakra

The seventh layer or the ketheric template is associated with this highest of the chakras, revered for its psychical representation of oneness with the one. It is the seat of enlightenment or the connection with the higher consciousness.

The crystals suitable for this chakra are amethyst, clear quartz, diamond and sugilite. Point the crystal downwards towards the top of your head, turning it in clockwise circles and again visualising white light.

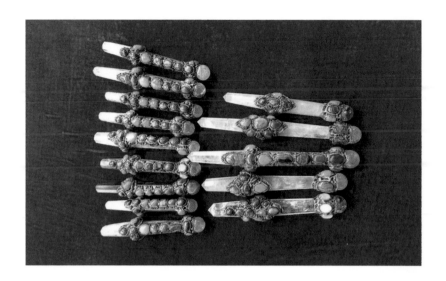

Crystal wands

A wand is a single piece of crystal designed for a specific use or a combination of various crystals affixed together to create a long tool for specific healing. Shamans and healers of a tribe often use crystal wands for healing purposes. To create a chakra wand we can take a wooden or long quartz base, to which we can affix crystals associated with each chakra in the same order as they exist on our bodies. If it's a quartz wand it should have points on both sides; otherwise, a single terminated clear quartz point is affixed at one end and a small crystal ball on the other end. This kind of wand can also be used for reflex or acupressure massage. A crystal wand can be used as a meditation tool, for aura cleansing and for chakra healing.

Chakra healing with aromatherapy and crystals

Energy healing is an intuitive work; integrating energy work with essential oils and crystals is very effective. The process first involves chakra assessment, which can be done via a consultation in which a client's case history is recorded or by using a pendulum, or by just using a palm to feel the chakra energies.

The next step is to anoint chakra oils at the chakra points. It is easier to apply chakra anointments to a client's back rather than their front, unless applying the oils to yourself. Use the middle finger of the right hand to apply the essential oil blend at the chakra point. Just use a single drop and rub clockwise, slowly and gently. Clockwise rubbing at the chakra points also activates the chakras, along with the essential oil's vibrations. As mentioned earlier chakra anointing should be done before meditation, and we follow the same sequence here with the application of chakra oils before a healing session.

Start from the ajna (third eye) chakra, then on to the muladhara (base root) chakra, followed by the swadhisthana (sacral) chakra and on up to the sahasrara (crown) chakra. Since we started from the ajna chakra, we do not have to do this chakra application again while moving up from muladhara.

Once the essential oils are anointed at the chakra points we use each chakra's selected crystals for healing. A set of healing crystals should contain one appropriate crystal for each chakra, such as lapis lazuli for the ajna (third eye) chakra, red jasper for the muladhara (base root) chakra and carnelian for the swadhisthana (sacral) chakra. For the manipura (solar plexus) chakra you have several options such as tiger's eye, citrine, pyrites or yellow aventurine; for the anahata (heart) chakra use malachite or green aventurine; for the vishuddhi (throat) chakra turquoise is good; and for the sahasrara (crown) chakra amethyst or clear quartz would be appropriate.

Avoid using tumbled stones, as they can roll over the body; flattened crystals (kabhushans) are more appropriate. Place the crystals on the chakra points in the same sequence as the essential oils application. Use the crystal to rub the chakra point gently, then leave it at the chakra point.

You can use a chakra wand to activate the chakra; otherwise, use a double-terminated quartz for energy healing. The chakra wand should have a crystal ball on one end and a quartz point on the other end. The body of the wand should have all of the chakra crystals sequentially arranged. Use the crystal ball to massage each chakra while placing your thumb on the crystal associated with that chakra. After that, use the pointer to activate each chakra. When using the pointer side to activate all of the chakras, start with the ajna chakra then go on to muladhara and upwards to sahasrara.

Please do not stop at the sahasrara (crown) chakra. It's better to do grounding, so bring the wand, pointed to the spine, slowly downwards all the way towards the feet, then take it all around the body from the left foot and ending on the side of the right foot, healing and sealing the aura.

Allow the client to stay with the crystal's energy for some time, during which you can also carry out energy healing. Once satisfied with the healing work, remove the crystals from the body and cleanse them before re-using them. For a practitioner it is important to keep your healing crystals set separate from your personal healing set.

Reflexology

Reflexology is a popular non-invasive therapy. Its philosophy and practice are similar to other zonal therapies such as acupressure and acupuncture. The hands and feet are the microcosmic representation of the whole body. A reflex is an involuntary muscle contraction caused by an external stimulus. Reflex zones are the terminal points or endings of nerves, and are directly connected to a distant organ or part of the body. The human body has a tremendous energy to heal itself; this healing energy surges through the body in specific pathways and could be tapped at different points: the reflex points. This simple technique helps us maintain good health, while reflex points activation can also help balance chakra energies.

Reflexology is not only a treatment but also a diagnostic indicator of diseases in the early stages. According to reflexology belief, vital energy circulates all over the body and between the organs, so if this

Foot reflex points

energy is blocked then the part of the body related to the blockage is affected. The energy blocks in our bodies are reflected at the hands and the soles of the feet. By using specific pressure techniques they can be detected and cleared through massage on the reflex points; this in turn has a definite effect on the internal organs. When pressure is applied on the reflex points the functioning of the corresponding internal organs could be rectified and regulated, as the reflexive action of the nervous system transmits impulses to the specific area. In reflexology, either pressure massage may be given over the tender point for one to two minutes or the pressure can be maintained constantly or intermittently; in all instances a beneficial result is achieved. Reflexology treatment is not a cure all, although it initiates a change in consciousness and the removal of neural blockages, thereby setting the ball rolling for self-healing. Multiple sittings provide long-term health benefits.

Chakras are an integral part of reflexology. As we find representation of various organs and glands we can identify the chakra points related to those organs in the same areas. Reflex massage on the appropriate chakra zone will help with healing and the balancing of the related chakras. The vibrations of each single chakra can also be harmonised and intensified through energy activation in the corresponding reflex zones.

The benefits of reflexology massage can be enhanced by using essential oils or specific chakra oils in the chakra zone. To initiate any healing sessions the therapist begins by activating the core trilogy of chakras; that is, the heart centre, the throat centre and the solar plexus. This sets the body's own healing mechanism into active participation. The knowledge, experience and intuition of the healer all play an important role in raising and balancing the energy.

Energy healing

The one thing that is undoubtedly universal among all of us is energy: it is the pervasive force allowing for life to exist and flourish. Frequency is defined as a 'measurable rate of electrical energy that is constant between any two points'. When there is frequency there is electromagnetic potential. We are being influenced by the magnetic action (or attraction) of the frequencies that surround our lives each day, and frequencies influence our state of well-being. Energy flows like water and finds its own level. Even by being in the presence of another person there is the potential for energy exchange, which explains why we sometimes feel drained when in the company of negative or jealous people or even sick people. Conversely, our energy gets a boost in the company of bubbly, enthusiastic people.

Since time immemorial energy healing had been practised by ancient sages, shamans, healers and priests who were able to visualise chakras and the aura. In recent times various forms of energy healing techniques have been gaining in popularity, especially reiki and pranic healing. 'Reiki' is the Japanese word for the transcendental spirit. In reiki, universal energy is used for healing and to clear energetic blocks. There are various stages of energy amplification whereby a practitioner acts as an open energy channel. This requires a high level of attunement, and the practitioner is required to go through various levels of practice to achieve non-doership (complete detachment).

Pranic healing is also an ancient science and art of healing; it utilises prana, the vital energy also called ki or chi, to heal the body, mind and spirit. The basic tenet of pranic healing is that a human body is composed of two parts: the visible physical body and the energy body, also known as the bioplasmic body. The physical and bioplasmic bodies are different aspects of the human body. There are two principles of pranic healing: the cleansing, and the energising of the subject's bioplasmic body with prana.

In all forms of energy healing it is very important that the healer themself is healthy and has true intentions of healing with non-doership. The healer is just a channel, like a water pipeline connected to the source; if the pipeline is corroded or dirty it will affect the quality of energy received at the other end. People can be born healers. If your heart chakra is open and you have love and compassion for all, you can develop your abilities and skills or learn from a master.

Colour therapy

Colour therapy has been in use for many, many years in different ways and forms. Colour is an experience, the result of the receptive abilities of our eyes and brain. Colours dominate our senses; we interpret our environment as much by its colour as by its shapes and sound. We all perceive colour differently because it's a form of energy affecting us at the mental, emotional, spiritual and physical levels.

Colour therapy works as the colours we choose in the everyday aspects of life have an effect on us at mental and emotional levels. Our affinity to a particular colour results from our needs, for the rebalancing effect of the particular colour. The seven colours of the rainbow are associated with our chakras as red-orange-yellow-green-blue-indigo-violet. They are the primary colours of the human vision range.

Red is associated with the muladhara (base root) chakra, which is aligned with grounding and the physical body. Different people have different interpretations of the colour red, but mostly it is identified with life. Red has a marked effect on our physiology, increasing vitality, muscular activity, blood pressure, respiration and heart rate.

The swadhisthana (sacral) chakra is associated with **orange**, which is a composite colour combining parts of Earth's red and the sun's yellow, symbolising the beginning of polarity at this chakra. Orange encourages joyfulness and is used to help fight depression and treat unhappiness.

Yellow is associated with the manipura (solar plexus) chakra; it represents ambivalence, power, insight and intelligence. Yellow removes security, enabling someone to take risks in life. It also increases critical and judgemental faculties, besides promoting detachment.

Green is the colour of growth and healing and is associated with the anahata (heart) chakra. Green is the colour of balance; since it stands mid-spectrum, it helps balance male and female energies.

Blue is associated with the vishuddhi (throat) chakra, and symbolises truth and loyalty. This colour has fresh, cool, calming energy and soothes nerves.

Indigo is associated with the ajna (third eye) chakra. A mix of blue and violet, it symbolises the end of polarity (ego) and unity (self). It calms the body and balances the mind, encouraging purpose, prayer and meditation.

Violet is associated with the sahasrara (crown) chakra; it is the colour of spiritual fulfilment, inducing contentment and symbolising unification.

For chakra healing, colour visualisation with the corresponding chakra colour and simultaneous meditation on the chakra points is a powerful healing practice. We can visualise these colours and breathe each colour vibration into the related chakra, drawing in for at least five breaths. It is not unusual for some people to be unable to visualise colours in a particular chakra; in this case, intent upon the colour can work well. The safest and best way is to invoke abundant white light, which is freely available to all. White light is actually the most balanced mixture of all of the seven colours and the shades in between. For self-healing, invoking this beautiful healing light without mental restraints will work wonderfully well. White light works with an intelligence of its own, and is far more purified than our limited awareness.

In certain civilisations, the ancients understood the healing and rebalancing effects of colours and erected domes of coloured glass of individual colours. When the sun's rays permeated through the coloured glass they would shower the colour energy on the people inside the dome.

10
The last word

Through this book we have tried to present fundamental information about the chakras from a health and healing perspective. Most of the information has not been documented, but has been passed on from guru to shishya (disciple). Coming from a background of science and psychology, we both have been able to comprehend the energetic effect of our mental and emotional states on our organs and glands, leading to the progress of disease. Our background using aromatherapy with lymph drainage in our practice, alongside the individual experiences of our clients and an understanding of Hindu spiritual practices, Ayurveda and tantra, made it easier to weave it all together and provide a scientific understanding of this subject.

We hope readers will gain an understanding of and clarity about the chakras and the vital role they play in our lives. We hope healers will be able to enrich their practice by using the information in the book, and blend their skills, experience and understanding in their healing practices. We hope this will be the beginning of the journey for seekers as well as healers. There is still much more to learn and unlearn in the process of learning.

An award-winning advertisement on a meditation practice by a spiritual group states: 'Embark on a journey where you are bound to lose all your baggage.'

In this journey of life we are all carrying our baggage of material desires, attachments, greed, hatred, jealousy and anger. In our spiritual quest we all have to lighten ourselves up so that we can ascend to a higher spiritual plane. Chakras are best understood as levels of conscious awareness, not morality. Impurities also have to be understood from the level of discrimination, not morality; they arise out of desire, self-gratification and self-interest.

There is much more to life than fame, fortune, status, authority and attachments to things or people. All pain comes to us through ignorance and remaining blind when experience tells us something different. In the process of birth, consciousness dawns on us from a subtle to a gross level, then we seek to raise ourselves from gross to subtle to merge again with the source.

Hari om tat sat.

Glossary

Agni: fire.

Ahamkara: ego.

Ajna chakra: the psychic command centre situated between the brows.

Akasha: ethereal space.

Amrit: psychic nectar of immortality.

Anahata: the heart chakra.

Anubhuti: a spiritual experience.

Anulom vilom: to alternate (nostril breathing).

Apana: vital energy in the lower part of the body below the navel.

Asana: a steady and comfortable position of the body.

Astral body: the subtle, psychic body, finer than the physical body.

Avatara: divine incarnation.

Awareness: the faculty of consciousness.

Bandha: a psycho-muscular energy lock that redirects the flow of psychic energy in the body.

Bhajan: a devotional song.

Bhakta: one who follows the path of bhakti yoga.

Bhakti yoga: the yoga of devotion.

Bhavana: devotion.

Bhrumadhya: the eyebrow centre, kshetram or contact point for the ajna chakra.

Bija mantra: seed sound; a basic mantra or vibration that has its origin in trance consciousness.

Bindu: the psychic centre situated at the top back of the head; a point or drop that is the substratum of the whole cosmos, the sea of total creation.

Brahma: the divine spirit, Hindu god; creator of the universe.

Brahma granthi: knot of creation; a psycho-muscular knot in the perineum that must be released for kundalini to enter and ascend through the sushumna nadi. It symbolises the blockage posed by material and sensual attachments.

Brahma nadi: the most subtle pranic flow within the sushumna nadi.

Brahmin: a member of the highest Hindu caste, namely the priestly caste.

Buddhi: the higher intelligence, concerned with real wisdom; the faculty of valuing things for the advancement of life and conscious awareness.

Causal body: the body experienced in deep sleep and in certain types of samadhi.

Central canal: the hollow passage within the spinal cord. In the subtle body, this is the path of sushumna nadi.

Cerebral cortex: grey matter on the surface of the brain responsible for higher mental functions.

Cerebrospinal fluid: a cushion of fluid that protects the brain and spinal cord.

Cervical plexus: automatic nerve plexus in the neck associated with the vishuddhi chakra.

Cervix: the circular opening leading into the womb; the seat of the muladhara chakra.

Chakra: literally 'wheel' or 'vortex'; a major psychic centre in the subtle body responsible for specific physiological and psychic functions.

Chiti shakti: willpower.

Chitta: mind; conscious, subconscious and unconscious levels of the brain.

Coccygeal plexus: a small nerve plexus at the base of the spine behind the pelvic cavity related to the swadhisthana chakra.

Consciousness: the medium of universal and individual awareness.

Deity: a form of divinity; a divine being having subordinate functions.

Devata: divine power.

Devi: a goddess; a manifestation of shakti.

Dharana: concentration; continuity of mental processes on one object or idea without leaving it.

Dharma: rightful duty.

Dhyana: meditation, in the sense of intense meditation for an extended period of time.

Dosha: a body type classified in Ayurveda.

Durga: Hindu goddess; a personification of Shakti pictured riding upon a tiger to whom personal ambition is rendered.

Ganga: the river Ganges, the longest and most sacred river in India.

Granthi: one of three psychic knots on the susuhmna nadi that hinder the upward passage of kundalini: brahma granthi, vishnu granthi and rudra granthi.

Guna: one of the three qualities or matter of prakruti: tamas, rajas and sattva.

Guru: literally 'he who dispels darkness'; a spiritual master or teacher.

Guru chakra: another name for the ajna chakra, the eye of intuition, through which the inner guru's guidance manifests.

Gyana yoga: a path of yoga concerned directly with knowledge and self-awareness.

Hatha yoga: a system of yoga that specially deals with practices for bodily purification.

Hypothalamus: a portion of the brain that integrates temperature, sleep, food intake, the development of sexual characteristics and endocrine activity.

Ida: a major psychic channel that conducts manas shakti or mental energy, located on the left side of the psychic body; the 'ha' of hatha yoga.

Idriya: sense organ.

Ishaan: the direction of north-east.

Japa: chanting.

Janani: one who has attained spiritual knowledge.

Jnanendriya: an organ of knowledge or a sensory organ such as eyes, ears and nose.

Kali: a form of Shakti who arouses terror and fear; the destroyer of ignorance in her devotees.

Karma: actions or deeds, the inherent subconscious imprints that make a person act.

Karma yoga: an action performed unselfishly for the welfare of others and the fulfilment of dharma.

Karmendriya: an organ of action such as feet, hands, vocal chords, anus, sexual organs.

Khechari mudra: a mudra of hatha yoga and tantra in which the tongue passes back into the pharynx to stimulate the flow of amrit from the lalana chakra, activating the vishuddhi chakra.

Kumbhaka: breath retention.

Kundalini: latent energy.

Kurma nadi: nadi associated with the vishuddhi chakra. Its control brings the ability to live without physical sustenance.

Limbic system: group of structures in the brain associated with certain aspects of emotion and memory.

Lingam: a symbol representing Lord Shiva, the male aspect of creation; the symbol of the astral body.

Loka: world, dimension or plane of existence or consciousness.

Lord Shiva: archetypal renunciate and yogi who dwells in meditation high in the Himalayas; Hindu god; destroyer of the universe.

Mala: a rosary-like string of beads used in meditational practices.

Manas: one aspect of mind; the mental faculty of comparing, classifying and reasoning.

Manas shakti: mental force.

Manipura: the Sanskrit name for the solar plexus (literally means 'city of gems').

Mantra: a sound or a series of sounds having physical, psychic or spiritual potency when recited in a certain prescribed manner.

Marg: path.

Maya: principle of illusion.

Moksha: liberation from the cycle of births and deaths.

Moola bandha: yogic practice of stimulating the muladhara chakra for the awakening of kundalini. It is practised by contracting the perineum in males or the cervix in females.

Mool prakruti: basic nature.

Mudra: a psychic attitude often expressed by a physical gesture, movement or posture that affects the flow of psychic energy in the body.

Muladhara: the base root chakra.

Nada: sound, especially inner sound.

Nada yoga: the yoga of subtle sound.

Nadi: a channel of energy.

Neti: hatha yoga cleansing technique in which warm saline water is passed through the nasal passages; one of the shatkarmas.

Nirvana: enlightenment, samadhi; harmony between individual consciousness and universal consciousness.

Om: the underlying sound of creation; the mantra from which all others have come.

Panch mahabhoot: the five prime elements.

Parasympathetic nervous system: division of the autonomic nervous system concerned with restorative processes and relaxation of the body and mind.

Pashu: the instinctual or animal aspect of human behaviour.

Pineal gland: small pine-shaped endocrine gland in the mid-brain directly behind the eyebrow centre; the physical correlate of the ajna chakra.

Pingala: conductor and channel of prana shakti or vital force, located on the right side of the psychic body; the 'tha' of hatha yoga.

Prakriti: the basic principle or substance of the entire phenomenal or manifest world composed of the three gunas or attributes.

Prana: life force in the body; bio-energy in general; the vital energy that operates in the region of the heart and lungs; the psychic equivalent of the physical breath.

Prana shakti: pranic or vital force.

Pranayama: yogic practice of manipulating and controlling the flow of prana in the subtle body by controlling the respiratory process.

Prithvi tattva: the earth element.

Purusha: consciousness; the spirit or pure self.

Rajas: one of the gunas (levels of consciousness).

Rudra granthi: the knot of Shiva, the psychic knot within the ajna chakra that symbolises attachment to siddhis or higher mental attributes that must be transcended before full awakening of kundalini can occur.

Sacral plexus: nerve plexus in the back wall of the pelvis associated with the swadhisthana and muladhara chakras, and responsible for the functioning of the urinary and reproductive systems.

Sadhaka: a disciple.

Sadhana: spiritual discipline or practice.

Sadhu: a holy man.

Sahasrara: the 1000-petalled lotus or chakra manifesting at the top of the head; the highest psychic centre; the threshold between psychic and spiritual realms that contains all the chakras below it.

Samadhi: state of being above mortal existence; all-knowing and all-pervading state of being; the fulfilment of meditation; a union with the object of meditation and universal consciousness.

Samana: vital energy operating in the region of the navel.

Sankalp: spiritual resolve.

Sankalpa shakti: willpower.

Sanskar: family values or disposition.

Sat-chit-ananda: a state of inner bliss.

Satsang: spiritual guidance, discussion and instruction from a guru.

Sattva: one of the three gunas of prakruti; the pure or equilibrated state of mind or nature.

Shakti: power, energy; the feminine aspect of creation.

Shambhavi mudra: mudra name after Shambhu or Shiva focusing the eyes on bhrumadhya.

Shanti: peace.

Shatkarma: rightful action (good karma).

Shiva lingum: oval-shaped stone that is the symbol of Shiva consciousness or the astral body.

Shuddhi: purification.

Siddha: adept, yogi; one who has control over nature, matter and mind.

Siddhi: perfection.

Solar plexus: intersection of a group of nerves in the abdominal region; the physical manifestation of the manipura chakra.

Soma: a plant used by the Rishis of ancient India for the purpose of spiritual awakening and mortality.

Sushumna nadi: the most important psychic passageway. It flows in the central canal within the spinal cord.

Swadhisthana: the sacral chakra (literally means 'centre of taste').

Swami: one who is the master of their own mind.

Swara yoga: the science of the breath cycle.

Swayambhu: self-created.

Sympathetic nervous system: the division of the autonomic nervous system responsible for maintaining the physical activity of the organ systems and expenditure of energy.

Tamas: darkness; inertia.

Tanmatra: the fives senses: sight, hearing, taste, touch, smell, and the sixth sense, intuition.

Tantra: the ancient science that uses specific techniques to expand and liberate the consciousness from its limitations.

Tapasya: the practice of austerity; purifying the body of deficiencies and weaknesses.

Trataka: the meditational yoga technique that involves steadily gazing at an object.

Trishula: the three-pronged implement held by Lord Shiva; it symbolises the three nadis.

Udana: the vital energy operating above the throat.

Uddiyana bandha: literally 'flying upwards'; a yogic practice of pranic manipulation utilising the abdominal muscles and organs.

Vairagya: non-attachment.

Vajra mudra: contraction of the vajra nadi.

Vajra nadi: the nadi that connects the expression of sexual energy with the brain and is concerned with the flow of ojas, the highest form of energy in the human body (concentrated in semen).

Vasana: desires that are the driving force behind every thought and action of life.

Vastu: the Indian system of architecture.

Vastu shastra: the Indian scripture of architecture.

Vayu: refers to the energy associated with each chakra (literally mean 'wind').

Vedanta: the ultimate philosophy of the Vedas.

Vedas: the oldest religious texts of the Aryans, written more than 5000 years ago.

Vishnu: Hindu god; preserver of the universe.

Vishuddhi: refers to the throat chakra (literally means 'pure').

Vritti: a modification arising in consciousness, likened to the circular wave pattern emanating when a stone is dropped into a still pool of water.

Vyana: vital energy that pervades the whole body.

Yantra: a symbolic design used for concentration and meditation; the visual form of a mantra.

Yoga: methods and practices leading to the union of individual human consciousness with the divine principle.

Yoga nidras: psychic sleep; yogic practice in which we can raise ourselves from the mundane state of body consciousness.

Yoga Sutras: text written by Patanjali delineating the eightfold path of raja yoga, the systematic path of meditation that culminates in the samadhi experience.

Bibliography

Athavale, Jayant Balaji and Kunda Jayant Athavale, *Introduction to Spirituality*, vols 1-21, Sanatan Bharatiya Sanskruti Sanstha, 1998.

Bittlinger, Arnold, *Archetypal Chakras: A Path to Self-Actualization*, New Age Books, 2003.

Brennan, Barbara Ann, *Hands of Light*, Bantam Books, USA, 1988.

Frawley, Dr David, *Tantric Yoga and the Wisdom Goddesses: Spiritual Secrets of Ayurveda*, Motilal Banarasidas Publishers Pvt. Ltd, Delhi, India, 1994.

Frawley, Dr David and Dr Rasant Lad, *The Yoga of Herbs: An Ayurvedic Guide to Herbal Medicine*, Motilal Banarasidas Publishers Pvt. Ltd, Delhi, India, 1996.

Gimbel, Theo, *The Healing Energies of Colour*, Gia Books, UK, 2005.

Johari, Harish, *Chakras: Energy Centers of Transportation*, Inner Traditions, India, 1987.

Johari, Harish, *Dhanwantari*, Rupa and Co., India, 2003.

Maehle, Gregor, *Ashtanga Yoga: Practice & Philosophy*, New Age Books, New Delhi, 2008.

Melody, *Love is in The Earth: A Kaleidoscope of Crystals*, Earthlane Publishing House, 2005.

Pandit Gopi Krishna, *Kundalini: Path to Higher Consciousness*, Orient Paper Backs, 2003.

Ratan, Ravi, *Handbook of Aromatherapy*, Institute of Holistic Health Sciences, 2006.

Sarkar, J.K., 'Anatomical and Physiological Basis of Raja Yoga', Appendix 2: Saundarya Lahari of Sri Sankaracarya, Sri Ramkrishna, Math.

Sullivan, Kevin, *The Crystal Handbook*, Penguin Books, 1987.

Svoboda, Robert E., *Aghora II: Kundalini*, Rupa and Company, 1999.

Swami Satyananda Saraswati, *Kunadalini Tantra*, Bihar School of Yoga, India, 1996.

Swami Sivananda Radha, *Kundalini Yoga*, Motilal Banarasidas Publishers Pvt. Ltd, Delhi, India, 1992.

Taimni, I.K., *The Science of Yoga*, Theosophical Publishing House, India, 1999.

Uhl, Marianne, *Chakra Energy Massage*, New Age Books, 2000.

White, Ruth, *Chakras: A New Approach to Healing Your Life*, India Book Distributors, 2003.

Wills, Pauline, *The Reflexology Manual*, Healing Art Press, Vermont, 1995.